SOLVING
THE
DAVINCI
CODE
Mystery

SOLVING THE DAVINCI CODE Mystery

BRANDON GILVIN

CHALICE PRESS
ST. LOUIS, MISSOURI

Cover and interior design: Elizabeth Wright

This book is printed on acid-free, recycled paper.

Visit Chalice Press on the World Wide Web at
www.chalicepress.com

10 9 8 7 6 5 4 3 2 1   04 05 06 07 08 09

Library of Congress Cataloging–in–Publication Data

(pending)

Printed in the United States of America

Contents

Acknowledgments

A book, especially a first book, is never written without the support of a number of people. I have been very lucky to have the support of many friends, colleagues, and family members in this endeavor. Trent Butler at Chalice Press has been an excellent editor, working tirelessly to keep me focused and correcting my tendencies toward long, passive sentences. Likewise, Jane McAvoy has long been an important mentor and was a great advocate for this book. The ministerial and support staff at Central Christian Church in Lexington, Kentucky, has also been extremely supportive of this project, allowing me the time to write, adding supportive words when I needed them, and providing me with opportunities to discuss the direction of the book. I am also indebted to the "Taking the Bible Seriously" Sunday school class at Central, who helped me work out some of the central issues in *The Da Vinci Code* when I taught the class in February 2004. The Lilly Endowment, which has funded my position at Central for the last two years through its Transition into Ministry Initiative, has also been an integral resource in the writing of this book, as it has provided me with the freedom to write as part of my vocational exploration.

I have also had many good friends who have read over drafts, encouraged me when I was overwhelmed, and laughed and joked enough to keep me going. And of course, this book would not have been written without a good friend loaning me a copy of *The Da Vinci Code*. Thanks so much.

My entire family has always been a great source of support for me in my writing endeavors, and this book has been no exception. My sisters Amanda and Jane have cheered me on from the West Coast as I have written this, and of course my Dad, Billy Wayne Gilvin, has given me his support in his own incredible way. It has always been my most fervent hope that I am made of the same substance that he is. This book is for him.

Introduction

> *"And everything you need to know about the Bible can be summed up by the great canon doctor Martyn Percy."* Teabing cleared his throat and declared, *"The Bible did not arrive by fax from heaven."*
>
> (*The Da Vinci Code*, 231)

If it didn't arrive as a fax from heaven, where *did* the Bible come from? When were the books of the Bible written? Who exactly did the writing, and where did they get their information?

Well, the short answer is that we don't know for sure. But for the last several centuries scholars have been analyzing evidence, poring over old manuscripts, and honing their scholarly skills to discover a solution to this mystery. For the most part, this work has been done in relative obscurity. Sure, biblical scholars share information with one another, publish materials on their findings, and occasionally grab the attention of magazines such as *Newsweek* and *Time*, but for the most part, this subject matter has remained a veritable mystery to the general public.

1

But the publication of *The Da Vinci Code* has changed all that.

Dan Brown's thriller, an exciting page-turner with a plot that draws on the history of scripture, conspiracy theories involving Frankish Kings and the Vatican, and an esoteric theory that Jesus and Mary Magdalene had a child, has raised serious questions for people of faith about the historical accuracy of the Bible, the life and identity of Jesus, and whether or not the Christianity we know today resulted from a conspiracy to cover up the truth about Jesus.

Unfortunately, a lot of churches haven't known what to do with *The Da Vinci Code*. Most academics, pastors, and Christian educators have been quick to point out the many historical errors and jumps in logic on which Brown's mystery hinges, but not a lot of attention has been paid to the hunger that has emerged out of *The Da Vinci Code*'s phenomenal success, a hunger for a solution to the mystery of the origins of Christianity.

Since I first encountered the non-canonical gospels in college, I've always thought that there was something of value in them for communities of faith—probably not as scripture, but certainly as documents that tell us something about our earliest Christian roots. So not long after reading *The Da Vinci Code*, an opportunity to teach a short-term Sunday school class emerged, and I grabbed it.

Very quickly I discovered that the twisting plot navigated by Robert Langdon and Sophie Neveu was not the primary mystery with which people in my class were concerned. Weaving our way through the intricacies, inconsistencies, and insight that emerged from examining everything from shadowy innuendo about secret societies to scholarly theories about a hypothetical document named "Q," we discovered that Brown had left for us a mystery we hadn't anticipated. This mystery was about our own faith tradition, and we couldn't solve it by simply rounding up facts and evidence. It warranted careful examination of everything we have said about ourselves as people of faith since the first bands of disciples set out on foot to tell the story of Jesus.

Much of what Dan Brown writes draws from historical fact. Human beings did write the Bible. Many gospels were not included in our Bible, produced by early communities who considered themselves faithful Christians. The Bible was more than likely edited and *redacted* by those who collated its contents. Constantine did play an influential role in the development of early Christianity. Biblical teachings have been used, and even developed, by political and religious powers for their own purposes. But just as solving this mystery requires us to filter through the many claims made by our age-old faith with a critical eye, we must also do the same with Brown, evaluating each of the clues he leaves.

In this book I spend six brief chapters examining several of these clues: *Did Constantine write the Bible?*; *Was Jesus' divinity the result of a vote of the Council of Nicaea?*; *Were Mary Magdalene and Jesus married?*; *Did Jesus and Mary produce an heir whose bloodline can be traced to an existing European family?*; *Has the Church conspired to repress the truth about Jesus for centuries?*; and finally, *How do the stories of* The Da Vinci Code *and Christianity interact, and what do we, as communities of faith, make of them?*

In investigating these questions each chapter outlines a series of supporting questions and the biblical and historical clues that end in a conclusion. At the end of each chapter are study questions that may be used in a six-week group study. Group leaders may choose to spend the entire study session on these questions or use them as a point of departure for group discussion. The resources at the end of each section are for the individual reader to continue research or for the facilitator of the class to research follow-up information raised in discussions.

Of course, Brown raises infinitely more questions than we could discuss here. But I find, after spending some time reading Brown's book and engaging in discussions with those who took my class and with others, that the questions I address are the ones raised most frequently. In many ways, they are key to connecting Brown's mystery to our own quests for a faith, to paraphrase Anselm, that seeks understanding. It is my hope that in examining these questions, I am able to provide a helpful tool to others who have found intrigue in the question of Christian origins. But more than that, I hope it serves as a reminder that truth and myth are inseparable and that it is the quest for our own history that drives us to faith in the first place.

CHAPTER 1

Did Constantine Compile the Bible?

> *"Aha!" Teabing burst in with enthusiasm. "The fundamental irony of Christianity! The Bible, as we know it today, was collated by the pagan Roman emperor Constantine the Great."*
>
> (*The Da Vinci Code*, 231)

> *But as for you, continue in what you have learned and firmly believed, knowing from whom you learned it, and how from childhood you have known the sacred writings that are able to instruct you for salvation through faith in Christ Jesus. All scripture is inspired by God and is useful for teaching, for reproof, for correction, and for training in righteousness.*
>
> (2 Tim. 3:14–16)

Startling claims about the nature and origin of the Bible make us stop and think as we read *The Da Vinci Code*. These claims affect not just the somewhat esoteric story of how the church collected and determined the contents of the New Testament. These claims go to the very heart of Christianity— its claims about the person and nature of Jesus of Nazareth.

5

"The twist is this," Teabing said, talking faster now. "Because Constantine upgraded Jesus' status almost four centuries *after* Jesus' death, thousands of documents already existed chronicling His life as a *mortal* man. To rewrite the history books, Constantine knew he would need a bold stroke. From this sprang the most profound moment in Christian history," Teabing paused, eyeing Sophie. "Constantine commissioned and financed a new Bible, which omitted those gospels that spoke of Christ's *human* traits and embellished those gospels that made Him godlike. The earliest gospels were outlawed, gathered up, and burned." (*The Da Vinci Code*, 234)

As we read Brown's fascinating book, he forces us to ask central questions about the history and nature of scripture itself. Then we must seek clues that help us solve the Da Vinci Code mystery. The clues we seek relate to basic issues Brown raises:

1. Who collected the writings in our present New Testament? When?
2. What writings were left out and why?

To answer these questions, we must search in the complete tradition of the church and compare the clues found there with those intimated by Brown. Then we must decide what answers we individually and personally find most satisfactory. So let's get on the hunt for clues to the issues involved.

Collecting the New Testament Writings
New Testament Evidence
CLUE ONE: JESUS' AUTHORITY

The New Testament clearly claims authority for the teachings of Jesus, especially in two ways. First, Jesus claims authority over the Hebrew Scriptures as he says, "You have heard that it was said...But I say to you" (Mt. 5:21–48). Second, Paul and other writers cite teachings of Jesus to give authority to their own statements (see 1 Cor. 7:10–11; 9:14; 11:23–27; 1 Thess. 4:15; 1 Tim. 5:17–21).

The New Testament also shows that the early New Testament church self-consciously preserved and transmitted the teachings of Jesus (see Lk. 1:1–2; Rom. 6:17; 1 Cor. 11:2; 15:3; Phil. 4:9; 2 Thess. 2:15; 3:6; 2 Tim. 2:2; 2 Pet. 2:21). This preservation was through oral teaching much more than in writing.

CLUE TWO: THE SYNOPTIC PROBLEM

It's difficult to start a discussion on the creation of the Bible from the Bible itself. After all, the early manuscripts did not come with footnotes or a bibliography page. Scholars have relied on careful analysis of the biblical texts for clues, as well as on gathering outside evidence from such disciplines as history, archeology, and anthropology. From such analyses a solid hypothesis has emerged. This hypothesis gives credence to Brown's contention that the Bible did not arrive as a fax from heaven, but in other ways challenges his theories with some other interesting evidence.

Scholars find further New Testament evidence by comparing the four gospels to understand the mysterious relationship among them. Mark, Matthew, and Luke, known as the synoptic gospels (*synoptic* implies that they report events from similar perspectives), seem to share many of the same stories and literary style, while John is very different in tone, style, theology, and even in some of the details of the story of Jesus' ministry, death, and resurrection. In attempting to solve this mystery, many theories about the relationship between the gospels have emerged. These theories are based on the fact that Mark is the shortest of the gospels and yet most of its material is repeated almost word for word in Matthew and/or Luke. Some gospel material appears virtually verbatim in Luke and Matthew, though not in Mark. Finally, both Matthew and Luke have material not duplicated in any other gospel. We will briefly consider the most widely accepted theory of the writing of the gospels.

According to this theory, Mark is the earliest gospel, probably written no earlier than 70 C.E. Matthew and Luke come later, each borrowing extensively from Mark. However, Luke and Matthew do share sayings that do not appear in

Mark. This leads scholars to hypothesize that both Matthew and Luke used and quoted another, earlier gospel document or source of information as they wrote to their different communities. This hypothetical source is known as "Q," short for "*quelle*," from the German for "source." This "Q" document included at least the information common to Matthew and Luke but absent from Mark. Brown mentions the "Q" source briefly; however, he implies that Jesus possibly wrote it himself. While most scholars consider "Q" to be a document made up only of sayings with little plot and no birth or passion narrative, no evidence points to Jesus as its author.

Matthew and Luke each have sections that are unique. The material specific to Matthew is usually designated as the "M" source, and the material specific to Luke is generally referred to as the "L" source. Although one finds in John some stories similar to those in the synoptics, this hypothesis holds that the author of John did not rely on the same sources. The relationship between the gospels is illustrated in Figure 1.

FIGURE 1

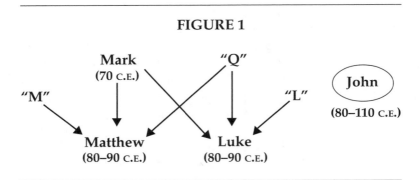

CLUE THREE: THE LETTER COLLECTIONS

The early Christian communities also passed around letters authored by important figures in the community of faith, including Paul, Peter, and John, along with some of their followers who, in the custom of the period, often wrote in the name of their teachers and leaders. These letters were read in the communities to which they were addressed and then circulated to other Christian communities (Col. 4:16).

Gradually they came together in fixed collections considered to be the authoritative letters.

CONCLUSION FROM THE NEW TESTAMENT

Brown's contention that the Bible has a very human origin and bears the mark of generations of editing is a very mainstream idea. One can easily find evidence supporting this in texts on biblical studies, or simply by closely scrutinizing the Bible. A diverse array of collections of authoritative literature began to emerge, reflecting the theological dynamics of each Christian community.

Early Church Evidence

CLUE ONE: THE FORMATION OF THE EARLY CHURCH

Following the crucifixion of Jesus, his band of followers was in disarray. One reason was that the first disciples were trying to make sense of the horrific death of their leader. His death was devastating and confusing for those who had put so much faith in his leadership. Even more confusing for the early disciples and for those outside their community was the claim that Jesus was resurrected from the dead. Such a claim had little precedence in the Judaism of Jesus' day. Though the resurrection of the dead was part of the beliefs of some Jewish sects, including the Pharisees, it was generally associated with apocalyptic thought. The resurrection of Jesus at a moment in history before the apocalyptic end time sounded strange, and often offensive, to ears more accustomed to orthodox religious understanding. The Bible says that this confusion miraculously turned to courageous certainty on the day of Pentecost (Acts 2).

CLUE TWO: COLLECTING PROOF TEXTS FROM SCRIPTURE

At this point, the only texts that the early Christians considered scriptures were, of course, the Hebrew Scriptures that we often refer to as the Old Testament. The earliest communities of disciples pored over these scriptures, looking for stories and prophecies that fit what they understood about the life and ministry of Jesus. The version of the Hebrew Scriptures many of them used is known as the *Septuagint*, a

Greek translation named according to a legend that seventy elders gathered in Alexandria, Egypt, to provide a translation for the Greek-speaking Jewish community there. These early Christian communities understood that Jesus himself had used all the Hebrew Scriptures to show that he fulfilled the promises and expectations that the Torah, Prophets, and Writings contained (see Lk. 24:25–27). In the Septuagint, these early disciples found many scriptures that they believed were relevant to—perhaps even predicting—the life of Jesus, including Isaiah 7:14; 9:1–2; 52:12—53:12; 61:1–2; Zechariah 9.9; Jeremiah 7:11; Psalm 22.

CLUE THREE: ORAL TRADITION BECOMES GOSPEL

Jesus taught in stories and in short quips that were easily remembered and shared among circles of believers. Very quickly the early Jesus movement developed a strong *oral tradition* that comprised sayings of and about Jesus. These believers thus preserved Jesus' teachings during his life and following his death. At some point, a new genre of Christian literature emerged. It was known as a *gospel*. The writers of the gospels collected these short stories about and sayings of Jesus and built them into a narrative that explained the importance of Jesus' life to the community to whom they wrote.

It's important to remember that gospels are neither biographies nor histories, at least in the way we think of biography and history today. Authors chose from the available oral traditions about Jesus and their understandings of what his life meant to address the concerns of the particular community to which they wrote. Thus the authors used the traditions of the church and told a story about who Jesus was and what he meant to a particular Christian community at the time each gospel was written.

CLUE FOUR: DATING THE GOSPELS

Another mystery surrounding the gospels is the question of when they were written. Many scholars assume that they were written no earlier than 70 C.E., based on a story that occurs in Mark 13, Matthew 24, and Luke 21. In this story, Jesus predicts the destruction of the temple in Jerusalem.

Because the destruction of the temple happened several decades after Jesus' death, scholars generally agree that this is not a saying originating with Jesus himself. Instead, they see it as a later interpretation that emerged after the temple was actually destroyed. Therefore, because this story appears in these three gospels, they must have been written sometime after 70 C.E., the year the temple was destroyed.

Just as many scholars see the real-life circumstances surrounding the destruction of the temple as evidence for dating Mark's gospel, they also see similar evidence for dating John. One of the differences between the synoptics and the gospel of John is how Jesus' adversaries are named. In Mark, they are named as "the chief priests, the scribes, and the elders" (11:27); Matthew points to "the scribes and the Pharisees"(23:2); in Luke, the adversaries are "the Pharisees" (12:1). John's gospel is filled with references expressing fear of or ire at "the Jews" (7:13). We can surmise from this difference that John was written much later than the three synoptics, as it demonstrates that the followers of Jesus had separated themselves from orthodox Judaism. John's understanding may reflect the painful expulsion of Jewish Christians from the synagogues, which happened no earlier than 80 C.E.

Clue Five: The Marcionite Controversy

The struggle for an authoritative collection of Christian literature actually began in the second century, not because of a mandate from an emperor, but because of the teaching of a now shadowy figure in biblical history: Marcion.

Originally from Asia Minor, Marcion is remembered as a heretic. He believed that the God of Judaism and the God of Christianity were not the same, and were incompatible. According to Marcion, Jesus rejected the religion of Israel, which promoted belief in an evil, bloodthirsty God referred to by Marcion as the *demiurge*. However, for Marcion, the ministry of Jesus revealed for the first time a different God—the supreme God of Grace.

Marcion claimed that following Jesus' death, the disciples, whether out of obedience to their Israelite heritage or out of their own evil intentions, "judaized" the story of Jesus, corrupting the actual story and compromising what Marcion saw as Jesus' rejection of Judaism. Jesus then appeared to Paul to correct the errors propagated by the disciples. Even Paul's attempts were met with resistance by the corrupt disciples, according to Marcion, who took it upon himself to purify the story of Jesus. He kept a revised Luke, in which no connection between the ancient Israelite religion and Jesus remained. He also added ten Pauline epistles. According to Marcion, this was the authentic collection of Christian scriptures.

Marcion's point of view was rejected as heresy. However, he forced the hands of many Christian communities and early church leaders; disproving his *canon,* or standard collection of texts, meant providing alternative lists of texts that represented the heart of Christian teachings.

CLUE SIX: THE PROCESS OF CANONIZATION

Slowly and informally, these communities began forging canons of their own, and as these communities exchanged correspondence with one another, consistency and consensus began to emerge. Although this was purely an informal process, scholars have developed a list of operative criteria that the churches must have used consciously or subconsciously in the selection of texts for the canon:

1. The text had to have been in widespread use among Christians. The less widespread its use, the less authoritative the text became or was assumed to be.

2. The text had to have some connection to one of the original witnesses of Jesus: the disciples or Paul. For example, Ignatius, the second bishop of Antioch, wrote seven letters to the churches about 110 C.E., and Polycarp, Bishop of Smyrna during the second century, collected the letters, which many saw as authoritative. But Ignatius himself wrote: "I do not order you as did Peter and Paul, for they were apostles." Closely tied to apostolicity is evidence for early dating. The Muratorian Fragment, with its list of canonical books from about 300 C.E., rejected *The Shepherd of Hermas*

because "it was written very recently in our times in the city of Rome." But 1 Clement could be defended by referring to its author as the "apostle Clement" and noting, as early Church historian Eusebius did, that it was read in the worship assemblies of many churches "in the old days and in our own time."

On the other hand, this did not necessarily mean that each accepted book that was attached to the name of a particular disciple was *actually* written by that disciple. In fact, often it was not the case. Mark was certainly not an apostle, but his work was connected to Peter. This is seen in a quotation from Papias, bishop of Hierapolis about 100 C.E., who says, "Mark, having become the interpreter of Peter wrote down accurately everything that he remembered... taking care not to omit anything he heard nor to set down any false statement therein." Similarly, Luke was not an apostle but was closely tied to Paul. It was apparently customary for Christian communities to adopt a disciple as a representative or patron, as their authority leant credence to the propagation of a gospel. Many of the letters ascribed to Paul were apparently written by his later followers. Scholars see this especially with regard to Ephesians, Colossians, 1 and 2 Timothy, and Titus. Hebrews was associated with Paul early, but is clearly not Pauline. However, the name of a disciple attached to a gospel did not guarantee the gospel's inclusion in the canon. Many of the non-canonical gospels discovered over the last century have been ascribed to disciples such as Peter, Thomas, or Philip.

3. The gospel had to conform to "the rule of faith." In other words, the work had to conform to the preaching and teaching that existed in orthodox Christian communities. Summaries and confessions of faith, such as 1 Corinthians 11:23–26 and 15:1–11 were often used as standards.

CONCLUSION: A SLOW, CONTROVERSIAL PROCESS IN THE LIFE OF THE CHURCH

Lots of controversy surrounded this process. Again, it was a slow, informal process that scholars can reconstruct only by sifting through the evidence long after the process was completed. Different communities used different books and collections of books as authoritative. Many books were met with resistance and debated fiercely. The gospel of John, for example, was unique enough that it was almost rejected. The letter to the Hebrews and the book of Revelation were also hotly contested. Still, by about 200 C.E. Irenaeus could write: "All who represent the aspects of the gospel as being either more or fewer than four are vain, unlearned, and audacious." By about this time much of the church agreed on the fourfold gospel and the collection of Pauline letters. Eusebius, writing about the time of Constantine, divided books into "acknowledged"—four gospels, Acts, letters of Paul, 1 John, 1 Peter, and, "if it seems desirable," Revelation; "disputed" and "spurious"—James, Jude, 2 Peter, 2 and 3 John, *Acts of Paul, Shepherd of Hermas, Apocalypse of Peter, Epistle of Barnabas, Didache,* and, "if this view prevail," Revelation; and the "fabrications of heretics"—*The Gospel of Peter, The Gospel of Thomas, The Gospel of Matthias,* and *Acts of Andrew and John.*

Still, only in the Easter Letter from Athanasius, Bishop of Alexandria, dated 367 C.E., thirty years after the death of Constantine, do we find the first official list that matches our New Testament canon. However, the controversy surrounding canonization did not die down for another century and a half, by which time the twenty-seven books we presently use became accepted as standard Christian scriptures—*almost two hundred years after Constantine's death* and *certainly not because Constantine collated the Bible.*

Writings Left Out

In *The Da Vinci Code,* Teabing asserts that the truth about Jesus' life is contained in gospels that were suppressed in order to meet Constantine's religious and political agenda:

> "Fortunately for historians," Teabing said, "some of the gospels that Constantine attempted to eradicate managed to survive. The Dead Sea Scrolls were found in the 1950s hidden in a cave near Qumran in the

Judean desert. And, of course, the Coptic Scrolls in 1945 at Nag Hammadi. In addition to telling the true Grail story, these documents speak of Christ's ministry in very human terms." (*The Da Vinci Code*, 234)

New Testament Evidence

CLUE ONE: MENTION OF NON-CANONICAL LITERATURE

The New Testament gives clear evidence of writings not incorporated into the canon. Paul wrote a letter to Laodicea (Col. 4:16). Luke knew of many accounts of Jesus' life and teachings (Lk. 1:1). Paul wrote a letter to Corinth before 1 Corinthians (1 Cor. 5:9) and a distressing letter to the Corinthians (2 Cor. 7:8). These were not preserved unless they have been incorporated into the other Corinthian correspondence.

CLUE TWO: NEW TESTAMENT OPPOSITION

Opponents plagued Paul and the other apostles wherever they went. The New Testament labels these as "false apostles" (2 Cor. 11:13) who preached "another Jesus" (2 Cor. 11:4). They wanted "letters of recommendation" (2 Cor. 3:1). Throughout the New Testament letters and apocalyptic texts, the reader finds references to such opponents of the New Testament authors. Many such "opponents" belonged to the Christian movement. One can expect that their opposition used the same communication tools that Paul and others used to oppose them, including written letters. Yet such anti-apostolic materials do not appear in the New Testament.

CONCLUSION FROM THE NEW TESTAMENT

The biblical writers were not the only people producing literature in the name of Jesus and his church. A variety of schools of thought developed in the early Church. Their points of view were widely debated and hotly contested. Even some materials authored by biblical writers such as Paul did not make their way into the final canon. The canon is a small selection of early Christian literature, not a full collection.

Early Church Evidence

Clue One: Early Non-canonical Literature in the Church

The early church valued many pieces of literature. The Muratorian Fragment apparently accepted the Wisdom of Solomon and the *Apocalypse of Peter*. It does not mention James, 1 and 2 Peter, and 3 John. Several gospels were known in various parts of the church. These included *The Gospel of Thomas, The Gospel of Peter, The Gospel of the Hebrews, The Gospel of the Egyptians, Dialogue of the Savior,* and *The Apocryphon of James.* Again, as we have previously concluded, canonization was more of an organic process that gradually happened, and many texts were considered authoritative at different times by different communities.

Clue Two: Lack of Evidence from the Dead Sea Scrolls

The Dead Sea Scrolls, contrary to Brown's statements, do not have anything to do with the life of Jesus. Found at the ruins of Qumran on the western side of the Dead Sea, these scrolls are thought to have been produced by a Jewish community known as *Essenes,* who were roughly contemporary with Jesus. Their community and its documents, however, have roots between fifty and two hundred years before Jesus. Some scholars have even posited that Jesus was an Essene, based on the similarities between Essene and early Christian communal practices, rituals of eating, and ceremonial bathing for purity. The Dead Sea Scrolls do contain important copies of the Hebrew Scriptures and are of great importance in determining the original text of the Hebrew Bible.

Clue Three: Evidence from Nag Hammadi

In 1945, an Egyptian peasant named Muhammad Ali al-Samman discovered a red earthenware jar that contained thirteen *Codices* (leatherbound papyrus books) of ancient Christian writings. Some of these documents were sold on the antiquities black market, and soon their existence came to the attention of biblical scholars. Eventually, fifty-two of the writings made their way to the hands of scholars investigating early Christian origins.

Most scholars agree that the documents found at Nag Hammadi were written around 350–400 C.E. However, these documents are Coptic copies of documents originally written in Greek. This has lead to much debate over when the Greek originals may have been written. Some assume that, as heretical documents, they must have been written later than those accepted as orthodox. Many scholars, however, date *The Gospel of Thomas,* one of the documents found at Nag Hammadi, as early as 50 C.E., which could make it older than Mark, and perhaps even contemporary with the writings of Paul. Needless to say, finding consensus on the dates of these documents is a difficult venture.

But what of the gospels recovered at Nag Hammadi? Even if they weren't burned by order of an autocratic emperor, these teachings were considered heretical or at least irrelevant by authorities within the church and were lost for centuries until they were uncovered by accident. What do they contain that made them so controversial—perhaps even dangerous? Are they, as the character Leigh Teabing proposes in *The Da Vinci Code,* the most authentic witnesses to the life of Jesus? Would their distribution uncover the secret held by the Vatican for so long? If so, is that really why they are not in the Bible?

It's important to keep in mind that the texts found at Nag Hammadi are generally described as gnostic. The word *gnostic* derives from *gnosis,* the Greek word for knowledge. Though there were many Christian Gnostics, gnosticism was not merely a Christian phenomenon. Rather, gnosticism cast a wide cultural influence in the early Greco-Roman world. Gnosis is not factual, informational knowledge. It is, instead, an esoteric, secret knowledge that an individual gains from a direct encounter with the divine. This secret knowledge can lead to spiritual release from the trappings of the physical, material world, which was thought to be illusory or even evil. Gnostic texts, therefore, were believed to offer secret revelations that would allow access to these direct, hidden truths that would free the properly initiated reader from the trappings of earthly existence.

Gnostic texts used complex symbolism to express their secret teachings. They often read like codes that would have been understood only by people already familiar with the theology of a gnostic community. Christian gnostic texts, therefore, would draw on stories, figures, and concepts from the Christian tradition to encode secret teachings. For example, one finds in *The Gospel of Philip* (estimated to be a third-century document) a teaching that seems to tell us something about the relationship of Jesus and Mary Magdalene:

> There were three who always walked with the Lord: Mary, his mother and her sister and Magdalene, whom they call his lover. A Mary is his sister and his mother and his lover. (v. 32, numbering from Bart Ehrman)

At first glance and in isolation from the rest of the text, this appears to be a historical claim about the life of Jesus. But it must be read in the context of the rest of *The Gospel of Philip*. This gospel is filled with other esoteric teachings, including the assertion that "'Jesus' is a secret name, while 'Christ' is a revealed name" (v. 19). *The Gospel of Philip* also claims that "In the Kingdom of Heaven the clothes are worth more than those who have put them on" (v. 24). For the initiated believer, such statements had several interpretive layers. While it may reflect an actual claim about the relationship between Mary Magdalene and Jesus, *The Gospel of Philip* more likely reflects a host of other beliefs. Words such as *mother, lover,* and *sister* may have also referred to metaphysical categories that were lost with the end of the community that produced *The Gospel of Philip*. Remember, for many gnostic groups, the material, historical world was illusory, and spiritual truth derived directly from divine sources was what was important. For the Christian Gnostic, therefore, the most important teachings would come from revelations from the *resurrected Christ* who has transcended the material world, not from the Jesus of history. Gnostic gospels, therefore, were believed to record teachings that came from Jesus following the resurrection. Because of this, one could safely say that gnostic documents feature much less, if any, biographical material about the life of Jesus than the canonical gospels.

Conclusion

Do these lost documents provide solutions to the mysteries surrounding the life of Jesus? Or do they just raise more questions? Brown is correct in saying that in this process, certain ideas and texts were suppressed and that surviving copies of some of these texts, hidden for centuries, were discovered in 1945 near the Egyptian village of Nag Hammadi.

Brown has done an excellent job of setting us up with a mystery concerning early Christian origins. He has left several clues for us, pointing us in the direction of the history of the canon and revealing the existence of non-canonical gospels, such as those found at Nag Hammadi. However, he has led us down a few dead ends by implying that the development of the biblical canon was Constantine's doing and that non-canonical texts such as *The Gospel of Philip* are actually more reliable historical witnesses than the synoptics, which were written several centuries earlier. The canon, as we have examined, emerged organically over several centuries, not because Constantine ordered its creation. It emerged in the life of the church and met specific needs of the church. The church gradually filtered out those materials that did not meet the needs of the church universal and did not prove themselves authoritative in the life of the church over the long haul. However, this does not mean that Constantine played no role in the development of orthodox Christianity. To examine Constantine's importance, we must again examine some of the claims made by the erudite Leigh Teabing, and we must also examine what was a pivotal moment in the history of Christianity: The Council of Nicaea.

DISCUSSION QUESTIONS

1. Do you think the synoptic gospels give an accurate view of the life of Jesus? Why or why not? Does the existence of other gospels challenge their accuracy for you?

2. What if Brown is right and the canon was influenced by Constantine? Would that change your view of the Bible?

3. What do you think about Brown's story of the creation of the Bible? Does any of his story strike you as feasible? Why do you think he changes some historical facts?

4. How does a work of fiction such as *The Da Vinci Code* influence or challenge what it means to be a faithful Christian?

Further Reading

Chadwick, Henry. *The Early Church*. Harmondsworth: Penguin, 1967.

Ehrman, Bart. *Lost Scripture*. New York: Oxford, 2003.

Frend, W. H. C. *The Rise of Christianity*. Philadelphia: Fortress Press, 1984.

Kelly, J. N. D. *Early Christian Doctrines*. San Francisco: Harper SanFrancisco, 1978.

Miller, Robert J., ed. *The Complete Gospels*. San Francisco: Harper SanFrancisco, 1994.

Pagels, Elaine H. *The Gnostic Gospels*. New York: Vintage Books, 1981.

CHAPTER 2

The Council of Nicaea and the Divinity of Jesus

> *"Jesus' establishment as 'the Son of God' was officially proposed and voted on by the Council of Nicaea."*
>
> *"Hold on. You're saying Jesus' divinity was the result of a vote?"*
>
> *"A relatively close vote at that," Teabing added.*
>
> (*The Da Vinci Code*, 233)

> *Let the same mind be in you that was in Christ Jesus, who though he was in the form of God,/ did not regard equality with God/ as something to be exploited,/ but emptied himself,/ taking the form of a slave,/ being born in human likeness./ And being found in human form,/ he humbled himself/ and became obedient to the point of death—/even death on a cross.*
>
> (Phil. 2:5–8)

> *He is the image of the invisible God, the firstborn of all creation; for in him all things in heaven and on earth were created, things visible and invisible, whether thrones or dominions or rulers or powers—all things have been created through him and for him. He himself is before all things, and in him all things hold together.*
>
> (Col. 1:15–18)

21

In *The Da Vinci Code*, Dan Brown emphasizes that the Council of Nicaea was an important event in Christian history. Many of the mysteries and secrets of his novel have their roots there. However, for us to understand those secrets, we must examine some of the clues Brown has left us regarding the council and the history that preceded it.

Convened in 325 C.E., the Council of Nicaea was the first of several early ecumenical councils, in which the Christian bishops were brought together to debate issues of polity and theology. According to the hyper-articulate Teabing, it was also the origin of the greatest conspiracy and cover-up in Western civilization. At Nicaea, so goes *The Da Vinci Code*, Constantine engineered the elevation of Jesus as the Son of God:

> Establishing Christ's divinity was critical to the further unification of the Roman empire and to the new Vatican power base. By officially endorsing Jesus as the Son of God, Constantine turned Jesus into a deity who existed beyond the scope of the human world, an entity whose power was unchallengeable. This not only precluded further pagan challenges to Christianity, but now the followers of Christ were able to redeem themselves *only* via the established sacred channel—the Roman Catholic Church. (*The Da Vinci Code*, 233)

Again, Brown has left us several clues concerning the historicity of an important event in early Christian history. But is it fair to say that the bishops oversaw a conspiracy to cover up the truth about Jesus when they gathered at the behest of Constantine in the spring of 325? Again we must seek clues that help us solve *The Da Vinci Code* mystery. This time the clues we seek relate to two basic questions:

1. Was Jesus perceived as divine before the Council of Nicaea?
2. What did the Council of Nicaea accomplish concerning the nature of Jesus' divinity?

The answers are complex, requiring an examination of both biblical sources and historical evidence. We will take the questions in turn and seek biblical and historical clues to help us in our investigation.

Was Jesus Perceived as Divine before the Council of Nicaea?

New Testament Evidence

The Bible does not present a single opinion on the divinity of Jesus. Although one would be hard-pressed to prove that any of the New Testament documents, all of which are much older than the Council of Nicaea, present Jesus as simply human, they do differ on the *nature* of Jesus' divinity.

CLUE ONE: MEANING OF THE CROSS

Paul's letter to the Romans, composed circa 50–60 C.E., does not focus on the divine personhood of Jesus; instead Romans focuses on the divine action that took place on the cross. For example, God is presented as the divine actor, and Jesus is presented as a *man* whose obedience reconciles humanity to God (Rom. 5:17). Through his obedience Jesus was raised from the dead and elevated to "the right hand of God" (8:34). Jesus functions as both moral and spiritual example for Christians to follow (6:6–11) as well as the one who intercedes on behalf of humanity (8:34). In this argument, the action at the cross elevates Jesus to his special status, not an innate or substantive divinity. Therefore, while Paul certainly understood that humans saw God through the reconciling action of Jesus, and while he certainly sees Jesus' Christhood as functioning as a spirit within the community of faith (in 1 Cor. 12, for example), Jesus is still a human whose resurrection leads to his divine status.

CLUE TWO: THE SON OF MAN

But what did Jesus think and teach? Did Jesus consider himself divine? Key in this debate is the use of the phrase "Son of Man" in the canonical gospels. "Son of Man" is a title that at some point in the church's history emerged as a title regarding Jesus' divinity. However, in the Bible, this designation has a variety of meanings. When this term appears in the Hebrew Bible, it's often a generic term that refers to humanity—sometimes collectively, other times individually. Many scholars see this as Jesus' own self-designation, while others believe this to be part of Jesus' teachings about a separate apocalyptic figure, similar to the "Son of Man" featured in the book of Daniel (7:13–14) in the Hebrew Bible. Still others point to the possibility that these sayings about the "Son of Man" were not sayings of Jesus at all, but part of the theology about Jesus that the early church developed. If this is the case, one can argue that Jesus did not perceive himself as divine—at least not in a way that used this term—but that his divinity was part of the thinking of the early church, long before Nicaea.

CLUE THREE: THE SON OF GOD

"Son of God" jumps out at modern readers from the New Testament pages as sure evidence of Jesus' divinity. As is the case with the designation "Son of Man," however, the use of the title "Son of God" is ambiguous. Such a title has roots in the Hebrew Bible as well as in the Greco-Roman world and meant different things, depending on the context.

In the covenant theology of Israel, influenced heavily by the tradition of *Suzerainty* (or Sovereignty) treaties of the ancient Near East, God was often described as a parent (Deut. 32:6,18–20; Jer. 3:4) while Israel was uniquely seen as God's son or children (Ex. 4:22; Isa. 43:6; 45:11; Jer. 31:9; Hos. 11:1). As the form of Israel's governance melded into a monarchy, the king came to be regarded as "Son of God," the representative of the nation before the divine parent and *Suzerain* (2 Sam. 7:14; Ps. 2:7; 89:26–27). This sounds much like Egyptian and Mesopotamian royal language, in which the king could be seen as a physical offspring of a deity. In the Israelite context, however, "Son of God," echoed no divine status. Instead, in Israel "Son of God" represented an important political designation that tied the fate of the nation to the king in the covenantal relationship with YHWH.

The Pauline letters use the designation "Son of God" three times. In Romans, this designation is conferred on Jesus because of his exalted status following the resurrection (Rom. 1:4). The other two uses of this designation (2 Cor. 1:19; Gal.

2:20) do not describe by what means Jesus comes to this status. While not using the full title, Paul does refer to the "Son" fifteen times.

"Son of God" is an important designation for Jesus in the synoptic gospels, though Jesus never uses it to describe himself. Demonic forces (Mt. 4:3, 6; 8:29; Mk. 3:11) and a heavenly voice (Mt. 3:17; 17:5) identify Jesus as the Son of God. Witnesses in the gospels also identify Jesus as such (Mt. 14:33; 16:16; 27:54; compare Mk. 15:39). Textual evidence on the opening verse in the gospel of Mark leads translators to differing conclusions, but most modern translations, including NRSV, include "Son of God" as original here. Luke accents his story of the birth announcement to Mary with the title (1:32) and uses the term in tracing the genealogy of Jesus to Adam, and ultimately, to God (3:38).

The gospel of John frequently uses the term in describing Jesus, and unlike the synoptics, places the claim on Jesus' lips as a self-designation (Jn. 3:18; 5:25; 10:36; 11:4) that leads to his crucifixion (19:7). John also emphasizes the uniqueness of Christ's Sonship: Jesus is the *only* Son of God (1:14, 18; 3:16, 18; compare 1 Jn. 4:9). John's stated purpose is to lead readers to believe Jesus is the Messiah and the Son of God (20:31; compare 1 Jn. 2:23; 3:23; 4:14–15).

Therefore, as is the case with the term "Son of Man," whether or not Jesus understood himself as "Son of God" is an issue fraught with ambiguity. The synoptics are generally considered more historical than John; thus most people assume that the fact that Jesus only refers to himself as "Son of God" in John reflects the fact that this is a theological designation made by early Christian believers and writers, not a measure of Jesus' self-understanding.

A story from Mark also raises the question of Jesus' perception of himself as divine. In Mark 10:17–22, a man addresses Jesus as "good teacher." Jesus replies, "'Why do you call me good? No one is good but God alone" (10:18). Is this simply a sarcastic reply? Does it perhaps indicate Jesus' equation of himself with God's goodness? Or does this point us to a clue about Jesus' own self-understanding of himself as human, offsetting the insertion of the early church's "Son of Man" and "Son of God" teaching into the gospels? This perhaps lends some credence to Brown's argument that the message of the early disciples diverged from the message of Jesus and perhaps included a claim to divinity that Jesus never historically made.

CLUE FOUR: THE PREEXISTENCE OF CHRIST

Another understanding of Jesus' identity from early Christianity focuses on Jesus as a preexisting divine figure. Paul's letter to the Philippians, written circa. 50–60 C.E., quotes what appears to be an early Christian hymn, asserting an understanding of Jesus as being of divine form:

> Let the same mind be in you that was in Christ Jesus, who, though he was in the form of God,/ did not regard equality with God/ as something to be exploited,/ but emptied himself,/ taking the form of a slave,/ being born in human likeness. (Phil. 2:5–7a)

This hymn apparently teaches that Jesus began as equal with God, emptied himself of that eminence, and, as noted in Romans, chose obedience and was elevated to an exalted status (Phil. 2:9). This hymn is widely regarded as pre-Pauline and points to an understanding of Jesus as a divine being (in some way) who existed sometime before his birth as a human.

Although its authenticity as a Pauline letter is often disputed, Colossians also understands that Jesus envisioned himself as existing before the rest of creation and participating in the creation process (1:15–17).

The gospel of John, written later than Matthew, Mark, or Luke, is an example of an early understanding of Jesus as a preexisting divine figure. In fact, John demonstrates the highest *christology* (or most elevated sense of Christ's divinity) of the canonical gospels. John begins with a prologue, heavily influenced by Platonic philosophy and very similar to the christological formula in Colossians, that asserts the preexistence of a divine Jesus, whose status was on a level with God. Jesus is conceived as an incarnation of the *logos*, a key concept in Platonic and Stoic philosophy. Essentially, in that mode of thinking the *logos* functions as a vital force through which the world is created and ordered:

> In the beginning was the Word (*logos*), and the Word was with God, and the Word was God. He was in the beginning with God. All things came into being through him, and without him not one thing came into being. (Jn. 1:1–3a)

Given that the gospel of John is usually dated as having been written sometime between 80–110 C.E., this points to a development of a complex theological understanding of Jesus' divinity approximately 220 to 250 years before Nicaea.

Evidence from History

Followers of the early Jesus movement needed categories through which they could make sense of what happened at the end of their leader's life. These categories weave their ways through not only the texts that make up the canon of the New Testament but also the debates and documents that emerged in the centuries following the gospels and the writings of Paul. Two formative cultural influences facilitated the development of this theological basis: Hellenism and Judaism.

CLUE ONE: BACKGROUND FROM HELLENISM

In Hellenistic thought, God was an unchanging, reasonable force that ordered the universe, but did not intervene in human affairs and was not responsive to human prayers and petition. Aristotle, for example, conceived of an "unmoved mover," a force that acted, but could be neither influenced nor acted upon. However, complementing this understanding of a dispassionate deity was the Platonic notion of a secondary primary being known as the demiurge, who came into more direct contact with humanity. These concepts became important themes in early Christian thinking about Jesus, including several scriptures we have already examined, such as Philippians, Colossians, and John.

CLUE TWO: BACKGROUND FROM JUDAISM

The God of Judaism stands in stark contrast to Hellenistic notions of God. In Judaism, God was not a dispassionate, unmoved mover. Instead, the God of Judaism was connected to humanity through fidelity to a covenant. God frequently intervened in human affairs, often reacting to the actions of human beings and changing the laws of nature, laws the God of Hellenistic philosophy maintained scrupulously. Judaism also maintained a strict monotheism, though from time to time one finds language that appears to depart from that, notably in the case of Proverbs 8—9, in which wisdom is personified in a pseudo-divine form, owing to the influence of—what else?—Hellenism.

Although Jesus exhibits signs of divinity throughout the synoptics, they primarily present Jesus as a prophetic figure in line with the Judaic tradition. He functions primarily as a rabbi and prophet who debates the law with his contemporaries, not as an incarnation of a preexistent God. However, we do see divine qualities in the actions of Jesus, such as the ability to perform miracles and healings. In the synoptics, at the time of resurrection—an action of God—Jesus is raised to a secondary, but divine, status.

CLUE THREE: ORIGEN'S SYNTHESIS

These two strains of thought—Hellenism and Judaism—remained in tension and sparked much debate over the nature of Christ and the trajectory of his ministry. In the third century, Christian thinker Origen proposed a synthesis for understanding these divergent understandings. According to Origen, the *logos* is the eternal expression of the Being of God, but is a lesser divine being. This being is unchanging and eternal, but closer to the creation and accessible for humans. Out of concern for sinful humanity, the human soul came to Earth in the form of flesh. Jesus was therefore an amalgam of the *logos* (a secondary divinity) and a human creature. Of course, reconciling this theory to the fact that in Christian literature Jesus is conceived of not as an amalgam but as a single being proved problematic.

Conclusion

The idea that Jesus had divine status of some sort had roots in Christian thought long before the Council of Nicaea. These roots come from the strong Judaic and Hellenist cultural influences of the time and weave their way through the literature of the period. Debates ensued as communities began to interpret what these texts meant, implied, and refuted.

What Did the Council of Nicaea Accomplish Concerning the Nature of Jesus' Divinity?

In the fourth century, two thinkers in particular set out to hone Origen's theory, taking the nature of Jesus' divinity in two distinct directions and igniting the debate that led to the council of Nicaea. Their names were Arius and Athanasius.

Biblical Evidence

CLUE ONE: ARIUS, HIS THEOLOGY, AND ITS BIBLICAL BASIS

Arius, a leader in the church of Alexandria, asserted a system that affirmed God as singular and unique. In this schema, Arius attempted to solve the problem that Origen set out by claiming that only God was unchanging and transcended all of creation. Drawing on the theology of Origen and John, Arius argued that the *logos*, though the first, perfect creation through which all else was created, was nonetheless separate from God. Likewise, as a creature, the *logos* was not omniscient and was capable of change and of choice. This led to the inevitable possibility that the *logos* could choose to sin.

However, in Arius's theological formulation, the *logos* chooses to be incarnated as the savior of humanity. Then through choosing to remain obedient to the will of God, the *logos* earns an even higher status and is permanently instated there by God. For humanity, therefore, Christian salvation comes through similar obedience to God in imitation of the example of the *logos*. Arius's theology relies heavily on his interpretation of Philippians 2:5–11, which does indicate that the exalted status of Christ (the *logos*) develops from his choice to empty himself and obediently serve humanity. Of course, according to Philippians, Christ is understood to be "in the form of God" (v. 6), which does not gel with the strident monotheism of Arianism. On the question of Jesus' divinity, Arius wrote that Christ was God through participation in grace. For Arius, Jesus was not made of the same divine substance as God, but was rendered God "in name only" through his participation in God's saving action.

CLUE TWO: THE RESPONSE OF ATHANASIUS AND ITS BIBLICAL FOUNDATION

If the Philippians passage is the theological starting point for Arius, then John 1:14, "And the Word became flesh and lived among us," serves as the starting point for Athanasius. For Athanasius, the *logos* was begotten uniquely by God, and therefore shared the same *substance*, a concept that draws heavily on Aristotelian thought. According to Athanasius:

> It is entirely correct to call Him the Father's eternal offspring…He is God's offspring, and since God is eternal and He belongs to God as Son, He exists from all eternity. It is characteristic of men, because of the imperfection of their nature, to beget in time; but God's offspring is eternal, His nature being always perfect.

Athanasius reasoned that for the *logos* to be begotten by God, the *logos* cannot be a mere creature. Just as human offspring share the same substance as their fathers, the *logos* must share the same substance as the deity that begot him.

For Athanasius, that God and the *logos* be of the same substance was not only of importance in describing Christ's nature, but also in describing the salvific nature of Christ. According to Athanasius, in Eden God joined humans to the divine word through their capacity to be rational, but because humans were created with free will, they chose to disobey. The stability maintained by this unity between divine and human was lost, and humans became corrupt and could die. The only hope, therefore, for corrupt humanity was for their human substance to be reunited with the divine. The only type of savior that could accomplish this was one who was incorruptible and unchanging, characteristics exhibited solely by the divine.

At the same time, only a human could communicate the message of God's reuniting action. Therefore, the savior had to be both divine and human, acting to stabilize humanity by uniting it with the unchanging goodness that is solely divine. Jesus therefore functioned as a new sort of Adam, in whom the created and the divine are reconciled, and through whom the fall of humanity could be reversed. Human beings, by obeying the teachings of Jesus and by mystically sharing of Christ's substance through the eucharist, could be reunited with the divine.

Historical Evidence

Clue One: The Nicene Debate

The debate over these two orientations raged. Arius, ever the brilliant propagandist, enveloped his teachings in popular songs that were shared by the working class. Both men spent time in excommunication. Each found their followers among the influential of the early church. As the debate grew in scope, many bishops added nuances of their own. Despite the fact that both positions appropriated the Bible to degrees of effectiveness, eventually only one would be established as the orthodox position. In this contentious atmosphere, Constantine grew sick of the bickering of the bishops and called the Council of Nicaea.

Therefore, if we consider the context of the long-standing tradition of Jesus' divinity and of the disagreement over Arian and Athanasian christologies, it becomes clear that despite Dan Brown's assertion, the key issue decided at Nicaea was not *whether* Jesus was the divine savior, but *how Jesus functioned as the divine savior*.

Ultimately, Arius's view was quite unpopular among the other bishops. Much of the energy of those gathered at Nicaea was spent attempting to define the faith so that Arian christology would be unquestionably unorthodox. In defining the faith, the gathered bishops formulated the *Nicene*

Creed, which is featured below. Of particular importance is one key phrase, which I have italicized. At this point Constantine was at his most influential:

> We believe in one God the Father All-sovereign, maker of all things visible and invisible; and in one Lord Jesus Christ, the Son of God, begotten of the Father, only-begotten, *that is the substance of the Father*, God of God, Light of Light, true God of true God, by whom all things were made, things in heaven and things on earth; who for us men and for our salvation came down and was made flesh, and became man, suffered, and rose on the third day, ascended into heaven, and is coming to judge living and dead. And in the Holy Spirit. And those that say, "There was when he was not," and "Before he was begotten he was not," and that, "He came into being from what-is-not," or those that allege, that the Son of God is "of another substance or essence," or "created" or changeable" or "alterable," these the Catholic and Apostolic Church anathematizes.

Solidly Anti-Arian, this creed condemns all those who—assert the creaturehood of the *logos*, and it insists upon Jesus' the *logos'*—preexistence. Despite his lack of theological acumen, Constantine insisted that the creed include the phrase *homoousios*, meaning that the father and son were of the same substance, a position with which many bishops, who despite their disdain for Arius's point of view were themselves heavily influenced by Origen, disagreed. However, because this position came from the chair of the emperor, they acquiesced.

Clue Two: Constantine and Nicaea

By calling the Council of Nicaea, Constantine heavily influenced the nature of the Christian understanding of who Jesus is and how he is divine, but to say that bishops voted on his divinity under heavily politicized duress is simply not the full story.

As for the history surrounding Nicaea, it is important to note that Brown's claim that the decisions made at Nicaea were "all about power" is not without some credibility. Although it was a theological argument, the debate at Nicaea did have important political consequences. Brown is correct in assuming that part of Constantine's motivation was to strengthen the alliance he had with the bishops and to establish some unity among different factions of Christian thought.

However, this political interest was not of the cynical sort, as Brown asserts. Constantine was by no means a sophisticated theologian. It is likely that worship of the Sun God was a formative influence in Constantine's upbringing. The jump from worship of the Sun God to Christianity was a fairly easy transition theologically. Constantine appears to have found in Christianity a religious tradition that would ensure effective divine patronage and the promise of the resurrection. Some scholars point to the name of his sister Anastasia (which translates as *Resurrection*) as proof of Christian influence in his formative years.

Likewise, despite Teabing's cynical assumption that Constantine's deathbed baptism was insincere, we should not assume that it was a halfhearted gesture. Rather, the rite of baptism was taken so seriously that those whose professions required violence, such as a military leader and ruler like Constantine, frequently did not receive baptism until just before death, preserving their salvation.

The emergence of the Nicene Creed proved influential for a number of reasons. It is still recited in a variety of forms in many Christian traditions. It became the normative formula for christological confession. However, the creed was not the end of the debate over the issue of Christ's saving work. Many followers of Arius continued to teach his banned teachings, despite its establishment as a heresy. The term *homoousious* would later be edited to read *homoiousius*, so that the creed read that the Father and Son were of *similar* and not *identical* nature, connoting that the Son was subordinate to the Father. Constantine, therefore, has had a lasting—though not thoroughly dominant—influence on the shape of Christianity as it emerged out of the fourth century.

FIGURE 2: Progression of Christology

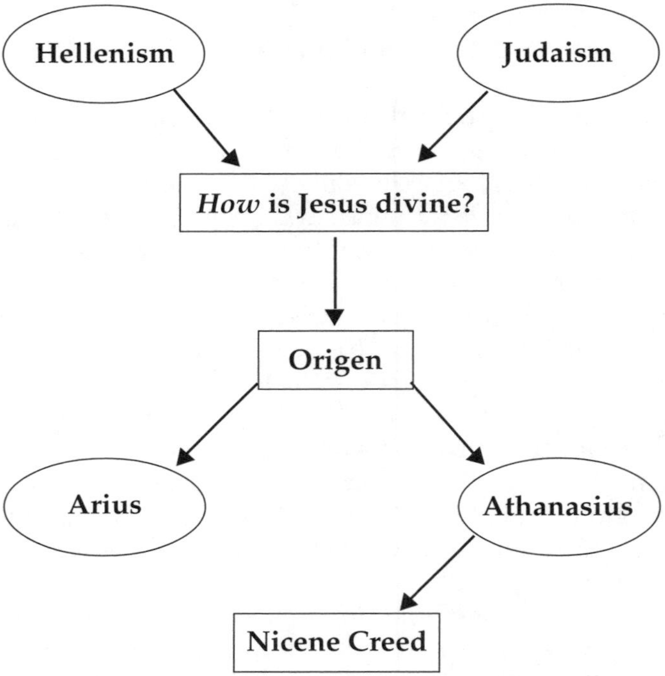

Hellenism → *How* is Jesus divine? ← Judaism

How is Jesus divine? → Origen

Origen → Arius

Origen → Athanasius

Athanasius → Nicene Creed

Conclusion

Again Brown has provided us with a mystery—what happened at Nicaea? Again we have had to turn to the clues he has left us, as well as the material we have in the biblical canon and in the annals of history, to solve that mystery. In viewing the contentious debate between Arius and Athanasius, as well as how its residuals played out in the forging of the highly anti-Arian Nicene Creed, we have seen the degree to which Constantine influenced the shape of Christianity, but even more than that, we see how he reacted to the issues facing an emerging Christian community whose values and theologies were developing in response to the symbiosis of culture and tradition.

But we are far from finished. In many ways the material we have covered in these first two chapters is merely the beginning. After all, the history of the Bible's formation and the history surrounding traditions of Jesus' divinity are simply background to what may be the most enigmatic mystery in *The Da Vinci Code*—namely, Mary Magdalene and her relationship with Jesus.

DISCUSSION QUESTIONS

---

1. What are the key differences between Brown's account of Nicaea and the historical account? Are there any similarities?

2. Do any of Brown's characters discuss the Nicene Creed? What do you imagine they might think of it?

3. Do you agree with Arius or Athanasius? Who offers the most solid biblical evidence for his position? Do either of their stances support the positions of Teabing or other characters in *The Da Vinci Code*?

4. Is there scriptural proof that Jesus was *not* divine? Do you see any differences between the synoptics and Pauline theology?

For Further Reading

Armstrong, Karen. *A History of God: The 4000-year Quest of Judaism, Christianity, and Islam*. New York: Ballantine, 1994.

Chadwick, Henry. *The Early Church*. Harmondsworth: Penguin, 1967.

Freedman, David Noel, ed. *Eerdmans Dictionary of the Bible*. Grand Rapids, Mich.: Eerdmans, 2000.

Frend, W. H. C. *The Rise of Christianity*. Philadelphia: Fortress Press, 1984.

Kelly, J. N. D. *Early Christian Doctrines*. San Francisco: Harper SanFrancisco, 1978.

Pagels, Elaine. *Beyond Belief: The Secret Gospel of Thomas.* New York: Random House, 2003.

CHAPTER 3

Mary Magdalene

Sophie said, "You think Jesus Christ had a girlfriend?"

"No, dear, I said the Church should not be allowed to tell us what notions we can and can't entertain."

"Did Jesus have a girlfriend?"

Her grandfather was silent for several moments. "Would it be so bad if He did?"

Sophie considered it and then shrugged. "I wouldn't mind."

(The Da Vinci Code, 247)

Jesus said to her, "Mary!" She turned and said to him in Hebrew, "Rabbouni!" (which means Teacher). Jesus said to her, "Do not hold on to me, because I have not yet ascended to the Father. But go to my brothers and say to them, 'I am ascending to my Father and your Father, to my God and your God.'" Mary Magdalene went and announced to the disciples, "I have seen the Lord"; and she told them that he had said these things to her.

(Jn. 20:16–18)

Peter said to Mary, "Sister, we know that the Savior loved you more than the rest of women. Tell us the words of the Savior which you remember—which you know (but) we

> do not, nor have we heard them." Mary answered and said,
> "What is hidden from you I will proclaim to you."
>
> (*The Gospel of Mary*, 5:7–8)

According to both *The Da Vinci Code* and the gospels, Mary Magdalene played an important role in the ministry of Jesus. But they disagree strongly on what that role was. According to Dan Brown's novel, the Catholic church has long suppressed evidence that Jesus was married to Mary Magdalene and that their relationship was not only a matter of historical fact, but of central importance to the very earthly trajectory of Jesus' mission. According to Teabing:

> It was not Mary Magdalene's royal blood that concerned the Church so much as it was her consorting with Christ, who *also* had royal blood. As you know, the Book of Matthew tells us that Jesus was of the House of David. A descendant of King Solomon—King of the Jews. By marrying into the powerful house of Benjamin, Jesus fused two royal bloodlines, creating a potent political union with the potential of making a legitimate claim to the throne and restoring the line of kings as it was under Solomon. (*The Da Vinci Code*, 249)

Is such a claim outlandish or feasible? That depends on the source being consulted, or the person being asked. However, when dealing with the character of Mary Magdalene, this claim is only one of several that are worth exploring. In this chapter, we examine her role in early Christianity by asking three questions:

1. Who was Mary Magdalene?
2. Was Mary Magdalene a disciple?
3. Is there any evidence that Jesus and Mary Magdalene were married?

These are questions that take us in a variety of directions and require us to look at not only the Bible but also non-canonical gospels. We must also investigate anthropological and historical evidence about the lives of women in the early days of Christianity. Although much has been written (especially recently) on these subjects, these texts and contexts remain mysteries as ready to be revealed as those in *The Da Vinci Code*. It is to those mysteries that we now turn our attention.

Who Was Mary Magdalene?

We know very little about Mary Magdalene. We do know that she is mentioned more often than any other woman in the New Testament except for Jesus' mother. We also know that her actual name was Miriam, not Mary, though we in the West continue to use this anglicized version of her name. Likewise, Magdalene was not a surname, but a reference to her geographic place of origin, Magdala, a fishing village on the northwest end of the Sea of Galilee. Outside the linguistic information surrounding her name, we do have a bit of evidence for who she might have been.

Biblical Evidence

CLUE ONE: MARY AS A WITNESS OF THE CRUCIFIXION AND EMPTY TOMB

In three of the four gospel accounts, Mary Magdalene is named among the women who witnessed the crucifixion. In all four gospel accounts, Mary Magdalene comes to the tomb of Jesus, only to discover that something is amiss. According to Mark, thought to be the earliest gospel, Mary Magdalene was with Salome and Mary—the mother of James and of Joses (which may or may not refer to Mary the mother of Jesus)—during the crucifixion (15:40). Matthew edits this event slightly, recalling that Mary Magdalene was with Mary the mother of James and Joseph and the mother of the sons of Zebedee, as well as many other women (27:55–56). In Luke's account, women are mentioned as witnesses of the crucifixion, but none of them are named (Lk. 23:49). According to John 19:25–27, Mary Magdalene was with Jesus' mother (her name is not given in John), his mother's sister, and Mary the wife of Clopas. Also mentioned is the disciple whom Jesus loved (the disciple whom Jesus loved is assumed to be a male figure, though occasionally readers of the Bible suggest that it may be a reference to Mary Magdalene).

In terms of the resurrection narratives, Matthew claims that Mary Magdalene and "the other Mary" encountered the resurrected Christ, then ran to tell the disciples what they saw (Mt. 28:1–10). According to Luke, the witnesses included not only Mary Magdalene, but Joanna, Mary the mother of James, and unspecified other women (24:10). In Mark 16, Salome, Mary the mother of James, and Mary Magdalene come to the tomb and find it empty. Unlike the accounts in Matthew, Luke, and John, Jesus does not appear in the resurrection appearance in Mark (at least according to the earliest manuscripts of Mark, which end with 16:8).

The gospel of John features an extended narrative, which presents Mary Magdalene, traveling alone, as the first witness of the empty tomb. Jesus then appears to her, though she initially mistakes him for the gardener. After this, she returns to the company of the disciples, whom she earlier informed of the empty tomb, and tells them of Jesus' appearance to her (20:1–18).

CLUE TWO: PATRON OF THE JESUS MOVEMENT

Luke 8 contains a unique story about Mary Magdalene and many of the other women who accompanied Jesus during his ministry. According to Luke:

> The twelve [disciples] were with him, as well as some women who had been cured of evil spirits and infirmities: Mary, called Magdalene, from whom seven demons had gone out, and Joanna, the wife of Herod's steward Chuza, and Susanna, and many others, who provided for them out of their resources. (Lk. 8:1b-3)

Therefore, according to Luke, Mary Magdalene and a variety of other women helped fund the disciples, though the uniqueness of this passage certainly begs the question of its historicity. Nonetheless, as a piece of evidence we cannot ignore, it raises the possibility that Mary Magdalene was a woman with comparative wealth and perhaps tells us about the access of women to financial resources and of their leadership in the early Jesus movement.

CLUE THREE: MERGING WOMEN

Several women are mentioned multiple times in the New Testament. Although many of these remain nameless, a number are named. Interestingly, many of them share the name *Mary*. Seven different Marys appear in the New Testament, including, of course, Mary the mother of Jesus and Mary Magdalene. Luke also tells us of a Mary who had a sister named Martha (Lk. 10:38–42). John tells us that these two sisters also had a brother named Lazarus, whom Jesus raised from the dead (Jn. 11—12). Mary, the mother of James and Joses/Joseph is also assumed to be "the other Mary" who is a witness of the resurrection in the synoptics (Mt. 27:56; Mk. 15:40; Lk. 24:10). Mary, the wife of Clopas, appears at the cross in John 19. Outside the gospels, Acts recounts another Mary, mother of John Mark, who hosted a house church where Peter sought refuge (Acts 12). Paul also refers to a Mary in Romans 16:6, encouraging those who receive his letters to greet her, for she had worked hard among the other followers.

Tradition has often amalgamated some of these Marys, particularly Mary Magdalene and Mary the sister of Martha. While it is possible that these refer to the same character, most critics and scholars separate them. Little evidence connects them, save for their name, and it is strange that Mary Magdalene would be referred to simply as Mary in one anecdote.

Yet another more problematic amalgamation of biblical women involves the woman "who was a sinner," mentioned in Luke 7, and Mary Magdalene, mentioned in the following chapter. Church tradition has often equated these two women, as well as propagating the assumption that the woman's sin was of a sexual nature, generally prostitution. In 591 c.e., in fact, Pope Gregory the Great delivered a sermon that conflated several women into one, including the woman of Luke 7, and assumed that they all were references to Mary Magdalene. Out of this emerged the long-standing tradition that Mary Magdalene was a prostitute who reformed her ways after joining with Jesus, though no evidence supports this, nor does the reference to her exorcism in Luke connote this.

NEW TESTAMENT CONCLUSION

Mary Magdalene plays as important a role in the New Testament as any woman other than Mary, the mother of Jesus. She supported Jesus financially and played an especially important role in the resurrection narratives. The New Testament says nothing, however, concerning a personal relationship of any kind between Mary Magdalene and Jesus.

Historical Evidence

CLUE ONE: THE NON-CANONICAL GOSPELS

Outside the biblical text, it is difficult to find historical references to Jesus that are contemporary to his life, much less references citing Mary Magdalene. However, she is mentioned several times in the non-canonical gospels. Though they offer little evidence about her life as a historical figure, they certainly inform us of her importance as a figure in many early Christian circles. *The Gospel of Peter*, discovered in Egypt in 1886, names Mary Magdalene as a disciple (v. 50). In strong parallels to Mark and John, it recounts Mary's discovery of the empty tomb. Widely used in the second century, *The Gospel of Peter* was later understood by church leaders to contain heretical teaching, which led to its abandonment.

A sayings gospel found at Nag Hammadi and hypothesized to have Syrian origins, *The Gospel of Thomas* concludes with a reference to Mary in a conversation between Jesus and Simon Peter:

> Simon Peter said to them, "Let Mary leave us, for women are not worthy of life."
>
> Jesus said, "I myself shall lead her in order to make her male, so that she too may become a living spirit resembling you males. For every woman who

will make herself male will enter the kingdom of heaven." (*The Gospel of Thomas*, 114)

The Gospel of Thomas is full of esoteric teachings, many of which find parallels in the canonical gospels. The key to understanding this reference to Mary, however, lies in understanding that many of the gnostic traditions encouraged members to seek a number of levels—often secret—of wisdom. These could be obtained within the course of study and devotion in the community. Gender could have been used as a symbolic designation for these levels. Likewise, given the illusory nature of the material world in the gnostic schema, the evolution of female to male in Thomas could be understood as a spiritual growth, though probably not a biological shift.

Thomas is generally understood to be a second-century document, though Elaine Pagels's recent book *Beyond Belief* raises the possibility that Thomas and John may have been fairly contemporary. She hypothesizes that much of John was written to refute the teachings and authority of the Thomas-styled communities.

The Gospel of Mary, which we will discuss more fully below, seems to point to a significant role for Mary Magdalene in the early church. She is featured engaging in contentious dialogue with Peter and delivering secret revelations from the resurrected Christ to the other disciples. However, the theological material in this gospel and its late date (debatable, but generally thought to be late second century), also show that while early Christian communities regarded her as a prominent enough figure to consider her a patron disciple and attribute a gospel to her, this gospel carries little—if any—historical material about Mary and her relationship with Jesus and the disciples.

CLUE TWO: DEVELOPMENT OF MAGDALENE TRADITIONS IN THE WEST

The conflation of Mary Magdalene and the sinful woman of Luke 7 may have happened as early as the writing of John, who in chapters 11—12 identifies Mary of Bethany as the one who anointed Jesus, though without identifying Mary of Bethany as sinful. This conflation had an important influence on traditions about Mary Magdalene in the West. Mary has for centuries been portrayed in art, literature, and film as a repentant prostitute who was not only healed by Jesus, but who also had her ways mended and forgiven. A juxtaposition of extremes emerged in the Christian (and Western) understanding of women. Mary, the pure virgin mother of Christ served as one extreme, while Mary Magdalene was imagined as the other extreme: a sinful harlot.

Of course, this dynamic between the two Marys has no historical roots and is anything but a helpful theological stance, especially in light of the influence of feminism in theology and biblical studies. Nonetheless, it is an image that is still perpetuated in many Christian, literary, and other communities despite the fact that scholars have discounted it for decades.

Was Mary Magdalene a Disciple?

One of the more controversial questions raised by *The Da Vinci Code* centers around the question of Mary Magdalene's position in the early Christian community. To ask whether or not Mary was a disciple begs the question, did *women* function as disciples in the early Christian communities?

Biblical Evidence

CLUE ONE: JUNIA

For generations, Bible students have claimed that only men served as disciples or apostles to Jesus. Often, in the popular imagination, the number of disciples has been limited to the traditional twelve named in Matthew 10:1–4, Mark 3:13–19, and Luke 6:12–16. However, the gospels make it clear that these twelve were not the only disciples of Jesus. It is also important to notice that in the Markan account of the call of the twelve, only the term *apostle* is used to describe the twelve, whereas in Matthew and Luke, *disciple* is used as well. Likewise, it is important to note that we cannot be sure if the naming of the twelve was an actual historical event. It may have simply been a literary convention that tied the followers of Jesus to the sons of Jacob, who also numbered twelve and are remembered as the heads of the different tribes of Israel.

Nonetheless, the designation *apostle* is not limited to the twelve named in the gospel call narratives, and as recent scholarship demonstrates, it is not a designation limited only to men. According to biblical critic Bernadette Brooten, Romans 16:7, contained in a larger passage of Paul in which he sends greetings to leaders of the early church, has been mistranslated for centuries. The name *Junia*, a feminine name, was translated as *Junius*, the masculine form, in most editions of the Bible until Brooten's research proved persuasive enough to cause other critics and scholars to support her claim. The *New Revised Standard Version Bible*, in fact, now reads "Junia." In Romans 16, Junia is described by Paul as "prominent among the apostles" and "in Christ before [Paul] was" (16:7). Much more evidence shows that women exercised leadership in the early Christian communities, such as the aforementioned description in Luke 8 and other references in Romans 16. The latter designates a woman named Phoebe as a deacon of the church. The reference to Junia as an apostle is, however, unique, and certainly raises the possibility that other women in the early movement warranted enough authority to be named *apostle*, perhaps even Mary Magdalene herself.

CLUE TWO: LUKE 8:1–3

It is difficult to determine what exactly this snippet of scripture tells us about the status of women in the early Christian communities. Quite possibly it tells us much about women's social and economic status—the women traveling with Jesus were able to provide from their resources, which intimates some level of financial autonomy for these women. It also possibly demonstrates the leadership roles taken by women in the movement.

However, as scholar Karen King points out, we must also be careful in assuming from this reference to women that there was as radical an egalitarianism in the movement as we might hope. This section could, after all, imply a division of labor in the movement along gender lines that elevated men to the level of apostleship and relegated women to the role of patron or provider.

Likewise, the fact that the reference appears only in Luke's gospel may mean that this passage tells us more about the role of women in Luke's community than in the ministry of Jesus. This passage may be based on the roles of and expectations for women contemporary with Luke, rather than on traditions going back to the early Jesus movement.

Nonetheless, it reveals that women *did* have an important role in the early church, even if that role was mediated by expectations based on gender.

CLUE THREE: THE APOSTLE TO THE APOSTLES

As we have seen from our examination of Mary Magdalene in the four gospels, she is consistently presented as one of the first witnesses of the resurrection, and the one entrusted to tell the twelve apostles what she witnessed. Her traditional title, "The Apostle to the Apostles," emerged out of this collection of parallel scenes.

For many critics and Magdalene enthusiasts, this proves her prominence in the early Jesus movement. For many it also provides sufficient evidence to speculate that more proof of her prominent role existed until the compilers of the gospels edited it out, though such an assertion would be difficult to prove.

NEW TESTAMENT CONCLUSION

The New Testament shows that women played a strong role in early Christian circles, even holding important "offices" in the community. The prominent role of Mary Magdalene could indicate that she also functioned in important roles in the early church, but such a conclusion is based on silence and possibilities more than on positive evidence.

Historical Evidence

CLUE ONE: THE ROLE OF WOMAN IN EARLY CHRISTIANITY

Women were afforded an important role in the early days of the Christian movement. Not only do we have the biblical evidence of Romans 16, but Christian sources such as Clement of Alexandria and non-Christian figures such as Pliny the Younger also refer to female Christians who served as deacons.

According to Rodney Stark, a biblical scholar who uses social-scientific methods, a number of factors raised the status of Christian women above the general status of women in the Greco-Roman world, thus attracting female converts. These factors include a ban on infanticide. In the wider culture, female offspring were often killed immediately. Although illegal, the practice was often culturally acceptable. Christian communities offered care and support for widows, and in terms of conjugal responsibility and rights, Christian women enjoyed much more equality than their Greco-Roman counterparts, who were often subject to prepubescent, consummated marriages. These protections proved attractive to many women, argues Stark, leading to a higher ratio of women than men in the early Christian movement. This situation afforded women substantial opportunities for leadership, and they took full advantage.

Biblical scholar Elizabeth Schüssler Fiorenza argues that this sort of egalitarianism between the sexes was a strong aspect of early Christianity that diminished significantly as the church became an accepted, then dominant, social force in the Greco-Roman world. According to Schüssler Fiorenza, "Women who belonged to a submerged group in antiquity could develop leadership in the emerging Christian movement because it stood in conflict with the dominant patriarchal ethos of the Greco-Roman world." However, as Christianity evolved into a more culturally acceptable religion, mainstream mores concerning gender roles were adopted from the wider cultural schema, significantly diminishing leadership roles available to women. For example, a portion of Colossians, which critical scholars place as one of the later epistles in the New Testament canon, features a household code very similar to those that emerged out of Aristotelian thought, which requires female submission to male authority (Col. 3:18–25).

This evidence, of course, not only opens the possibility that Mary Magdalene was among many women who experienced significant leadership in the early days of the church, but it substantiates Brown's claim that female leadership was greatly suppressed by the institutional church. However, *The Da Vinci Code* insinuates that the only force that sustained the influence of women in the church was the secret society The Priory of Sion, which, if it existed, kept secret documents that prove the influence wielded by Mary Magdalene in continuing Jesus' work.

However, as church historian Dale Johnson asserts, the earliest days of Christianity were not the only period in which women shared authority in the many varied strands of the church. In fact, Johnson argues that women made significant gains in leadership and authority in sectarian or countercultural Christian movements, especially those in which the authority of personal experience complemented the authority of the Bible, such as medieval mystics or the early Quaker movement. However, according to Johnson, by the third generation of a movement, gains made by women are almost always lost, replaced by a male-dominated institution that uses the authority of the Bible and tradition to limit leadership roles of women.

The important thing to realize, according to Johnson, is that the leadership of women has ebbed and flowed throughout the history of Christianity. Brown's assertion that there was a purely egalitarian beginning of Christianity that has been lost for two thousand years, though based in part on solid history, is oversimplified and ignores the prominence of women in many currents of Christianity, Catholic and otherwise.

CLUE TWO: *THE GOSPEL OF MARY*

The Gospel of Mary, among the documents found at Nag Hammadi, raises the possibility that Mary Magdalene was considered a disciple by at least some early Christian communities. If we hearken back to the criteria by which a gospel gained authority among communities in the early church, we remember that it was customary to ascribe a work to a figure who had a strong connection to Jesus—either Paul or one of the disciples. This leads us to assume that Mary was understood to be a church leader of significant status in some circles. Moreover, as Karen King argues, it is not only the eponymous title of this book that proves the weight of Mary's importance in early Christianity, but also its ending. There Mary, Peter, and Levi debate the legitimacy of Mary's leadership, reflecting a debate about her authority—*and the authority of women in general*—in later generations of Christian communities:

> [Peter] questioned them about the Savior: "Did he really speak with a woman without our knowledge (and) not openly? Are we to turn about and all listen to her? Did he prefer her to us?"
>
> Then Mary wept and said to Peter, "My brother Peter, what do you think? Do you think that I thought this up myself in my heart, or that I am lying about the Savior?"
>
> Levi answered and said to Peter, "Peter, you have always been hot-tempered. Now I see you contending against the woman like the adversaries. But if the Savior made her worthy, who are you indeed to reject her? (*The Gospel of Mary*, 9:3–8)

We find, in this text, a claim about Mary's apostolic authority based on her personal experience with the divine, a significant feature not only of gnostic Christianity, but as Johnson noted, a significant trait of religious movements in which women exercise significant authority. Although this text does not provide direct evidence of Mary's status as a disciple during her lifetime, it does tell us that there were communities that afforded her a status on par with that of male disciples.

Were Jesus and Mary Magdalene Married?

One of the most controversial claims made in *The Da Vinci Code* is that Jesus and Mary Magdalene were married. In fact,

Teabing claims that this marriage is "a matter of historical record." But is such a claim easy to substantiate? Is there any evidence for such a claim at all?

Biblical Evidence

CLUE ONE: THE JOHANNINE DIALOGUE

The biblical texts give absolutely no direct evidence that there was any sort of marital or sexual relationship between Jesus and Mary Magdalene. However, some critics read a level of intimacy into Jesus' appearance to Mary in John 20. They claim, for example, that her attempts to embrace him in that scene and her use of "Rabboni," a more familiar, affectionate form of the word *rabbi,* demonstrate a level of intimacy that could indicate a relationship between them.

Of course, two things about John are important to recognize in this regard. Namely, John is a highly symbolic book, and its composition is significantly later than the synoptics. This high level of symbolism and late date of composition therefore cast fairly significant doubt on whether this passage has historical merit. Likely, Mary's attempt to hold on to Jesus is more of a theological statement than proof of intimacy, as Jesus' reply seems to indicate:

> "Do not hold on to me, because I have not yet ascended to the Father. But go to my brothers and say to them, "I am ascending to my Father and your Father, to my God and your God." (Jn. 20:17)

CLUE TWO: ARGUMENT FROM SILENCE

Of course, nothing in any of the gospels denies the possibility that Jesus might have been married. The Bible is simply silent on the matter, though there are plenty of interesting references to family, such as in Mark, when Jesus is told that his mother, brother, and sisters are waiting for him, to which he replies, "Who are my mother and my brothers?...Whoever does the will of God is my brother and sister and mother" (Mk. 3:33–35). Matthew and Luke also emphasize that discipleship requires an abandonment of familial ties (Mt. 8:21–22; Lk. 9:59–60). There is also a strange reference to eunuchs in Matthew, which has traditionally been taken as a teaching on celibacy (Mt. 19:10–12); Mark and Matthew also include a teaching on divorce (Mt. 19:1–9, Mk. 10:2–12). Besides references such as these, nothing indicates whether or not Jesus was married. The silence on the subject has led to a wide variety of hypotheses.

William Phipps in *The Sexuality of Jesus* argues that it would be highly unusual for Jesus, as a Jewish male, to not be married. Phipps hypothesizes that perhaps during the years between his childhood and adulthood—years not recorded in the gospels—he had a family that was decimated, leaving "the dead to bury the dead." An alternative take on his family is that he simply abandoned them. This is difficult for us to imagine, especially given a predilection in our culture for a set of "Christian family values," but the references to leaving family behind in the synoptics certainly raise the possibility.

Of course, as we mentioned in chapter 1, the striking similarities between some Essene teachings have led scholars to believe that Jesus was an Essene, or at least heavily influenced by their teachings. If that is the case, we must consider the fact that Essenes practiced celibacy. That may provide an explanation for the lack of familial references—for early readers familiar with the community's norms, celibacy would have been a given.

Others, like Brown, argue that following the cultural expectations of the period, Jesus would have been married. This argument concludes that the original gospels were excised of all references to Jesus' family, either to protect them from persecution following his death or to cover up their existence in the church. Of course, some argue that Jesus' divine status—or self-understanding of himself as divine—would preclude any sort of sexual relationship or family relations.

New Testament Conclusion

The lack of concrete evidence about Jesus' marital status makes all these hypotheses viable, though to varying degrees.

Nonetheless, barring a significant archeological find, these possibilities will all remain hypothetical.

Historical Evidence

CLUE ONE: THE GNOSTIC TEXTS

Just as it has been difficult for us to pinpoint historical evidence about the life of Mary Magdalene outside the gospels, it is difficult for us to locate evidence outside the biblical texts that proves a marriage or relationship between Jesus and Mary Magdalene. Again the gnostic gospels provide us with a debatable bit of evidence of the relationship between Mary and Jesus.

The Gospel of Philip garners quite a bit of attention in *The Da Vinci Code*. Teabing claims this gospel offers the most substantial proof of the relationship between Mary and Jesus, based on verses 32 and 55, which on first glance seem to intimate that there is indeed something to their relationship:

> There were three who always walked with the Lord: Mary, his mother and her sister, and Magdalene, whom they call his lover. A Mary is his sister and his mother and his lover (v. 32)

> Wisdom (*Sophia*), whom they call barren, is the mother of the angels, and the consort of Christ is Mary Magdalene. The [Lord loved Mary] more than all the disciples, and he kissed her on the [mouth many times]. The other [women/disciples saw]…him. They said to him, "Why do you [love her] more than all of us?" The savior answered and said to them, "Why do not I love you as I do her?" (v. 55)

As we discussed briefly in chapter 1, these traditions likely reflect a Christian community's understanding of Mary Magdalene as more than a character in a story, but as a symbol pointing toward a greater spiritual insight. This is especially evident in 55, where her companionship with Christ is juxtaposed with the image of Wisdom (*Sophia*). Mary Magdalene seems to be understood as the vessel of divine wisdom in this tradition, which gives her a prominent identity in that community. However, its estimated third-century authorship casts significant doubt on any historical evidence that we might glean about Mary Magdalene from Philip.

Likewise, Levi's statement following the disagreement between Mary and Peter in *The Gospel of Mary* that Jesus loved Mary more than the rest of the disciples may function more as a claim about Mary's apostolic authority than about her intimacy with Jesus.

CLUE TWO: THE WOMAN WITH THE ALABASTER JAR

Margaret Starbird's 1993 book *The Woman with the Alabaster Jar* presents a multidisciplinary approach to the question of the marriage of Jesus and Mary Magdalene. In the preface, she recalls experiencing a severe crisis of faith after reading *Holy Blood, Holy Grail*, which propagated a hypothesis on the bloodline of Christ, an issue we will examine in the next chapter. Starbird originally set out to disprove the authors of *Holy Blood*, but soon found herself invested in their hypothesis. Her research takes *Holy Blood, Holy Grail* in a constructive direction, forging a theological statement heavily reliant on its claims about Jesus and Mary Magdalene.

Relying on the gospels, non-canonical texts, art history, and arguments drawn on hypotheses about cross-cultural archetypes and images of the divine feminine, Starbird believes that there is significant evidence of a long-held tradition of the marriage of Jesus and Mary Magdalene. This is as much a theological statement as a historical statement for Starbird, however, for though she concedes that there is no way to prove the historicity of her claim, she does believe that a restoration (or introduction) of Jesus' marriage to Mary Magdalene to the Christian narrative would restore a balance between male and female images of the divine, a balance that has been lost in the excision of that tradition:

> After nearly two thousand years, it is time to set the record straight, to revise and complete the gospel story of Jesus to include his wife. Our ravaged

environment, our abused children, our maimed veterans, our self-destructing families and abandoned spouses are all crying for the restoration of the Bride of Christ. (*The Woman with the Alabaster Jar,* 177)

Starbird's claims lead us to some tricky territory. While for her, historicity of the marriage of Jesus and Mary Magdalene is secondary to the theological and mythological value of a marriage between male and female incarnations of the divine, she is nonetheless making a statement of faith that requires a huge burden of historical and biblical proof. If we take her at her word, does this mean that we must read the Bible as theologically incomplete, or does it mean that we must read it as historically incorrect? And because it is a book that makes theological claims about events in history, can we afford to make a distinction?

The Verdict

As a figure from the Bible, Mary Magdalene continues to remain fairly elusive.

We are able to discern that she was a figure of importance to the early church, perhaps even important enough to be considered a disciple. However, there remains little evidence of an intimate relationship or marriage to Jesus, outside of documents from Nag Hammadi that seem to be more symbolic than historic in their approach, and outside of popular traditions that merge goddess traditions, folklore, and biblical narrative. Even Margaret Starbird, who has become a strong advocate for belief in the marriage of Jesus and Mary Magdalene, bases her assertion on faith rather than historical evidence.

However, there is a text mentioned in *The Da Vinci Code* and relied on heavily by Starbird whose authors claim it to be historical evidence supporting a hypothesis that Jesus and Mary Magdalene were married and that their marriage produced a bloodline that can be traced to contemporary heirs. It is to this book that we turn in our next chapter.

DISCUSSION QUESTIONS

1. Does the possibility of Jesus' marriage affect your understanding of his divinity? Can Jesus be both married and messiah?

2. What does it mean to be a disciple of Jesus? Does that title fit Mary Magdalene?

3. Is Margaret Starbird correct? Do we need a feminine principle of God? Is Mary Magdalene an adequate representation of that principle, even if there is no historical evidence for her marriage to Jesus?

4. What does Mary Magdalene's presence at the resurrection in John say about her role in the Christian story?

For Further Reading

Baigent, Michael, Richard Leigh, and Henry Lincoln. *Holy Blood, Holy Grail*. New York: Dell, 1983.

Brooten, Bernadette. "Junia...Outstanding among the Apostles (Rom. 16:7)." In *Women Priests*, edited by Arlene Swidler and Leonard Swidler. New York: Paulist Press, 1977.

King, Karen. *The Gospel of Mary of Magdala*. Santa Rosa, Calif.: Polebridge, 2003.

Meyers, Carol, ed. *Women in Scripture*. Boston: Houghton Mifflin, 2000.

Phipps, William. *The Sexuality of Jesus*. Cleveland: Pilgrim Press, 1996.

Schüssler Fiorenza, Elisabeth. *In Memory of Her*. Tenth Anniversary Edition. New York: Crossroad, 1994.

Starbird, Margaret. *The Woman with the Alabaster Jar*. Santa Fe, N.M.: Bear and Company, 1993.

Stark, Rodney. *The Rise of Christianity*. San Francisco: Harper SanFrancisco, 1997.

CHAPTER 4

Did Jesus and Mary Produce an Heir?

"Here is perhaps the best-known tome," Teabing said, pulling a tattered hardcover from the stack and handing it to her.

The cover read:

HOLY BLOOD, HOLY GRAIL
The Acclaimed International Bestseller

Sophie glanced up. "An international bestseller? I've never heard of it."

(*The Da Vinci Code*, 253)

If our Hypothesis is correct, Jesus' wife and offspring, (and he could have fathered a number of children between the ages of 16 or 17 and his supposed death), after fleeing the Holy Land, found refuge in the south of France, and in a Jewish community there preserve their lineage. During the fifth century this lineage appears to have intermarried with the royal line of Franks, thus engendering the Merovingian dynasty.

(*Holy Blood, Holy Grail*, 400)

Then Pilate entered the headquarters again, summoned Jesus, and asked him, "Are you the King of the Jews?"...

57

Jesus answered, "My kingdom is not from this world. If my kingdom were from this world, my followers would be fighting to keep me from being handed over to the Jews. But as it is, my kingdom is not from here." Pilate asked him, "So you are a king?" Jesus answered, "You say that I am a king. For this I was born, and for this I came into the world, to testify to the truth. Everyone who belongs to the truth listens to my voice." Pilate asked him, "What is truth?"

(Jn. 18:33, 36–38a)

Opening *The Da Vinci Code*, one finds an introductory page with the following inscription:

Fact:

The Priory of Sion—a European secret society founded in 1099—is a real organization.

In 1975 Paris's Bibliotheque Nationale discovered parchments known as *Les Dossiers Secrets*, identifying numerous members of the Priory of Sion, including Sir Isaac Newton, Botticelli, Victor Hugo, and Leonardo da Vinci.

A fascinating assertion! As we know, The Priory of Sion plays a key role in *The Da Vinci Code*, but is their existence, and furthermore their mission as purported in Brown's novel, factual? Brown is clearly basing his assertion on the hypothesis put forth by Michael Baigent, Richard Leigh, and Henry Lincoln in their bestseller from the early 1980s, *Holy Blood, Holy Grail*.

For the sake of storytelling, Brown does deviate a bit from the scenario put forth by *Holy Blood, Holy Grail*, but clearly its alternative account of the development of Christianity in early Palestine and in Europe plays an important role in the development of Brown's cast of characters, plot, and theological schema. But does Brown's appropriation of *Holy Blood, Holy Grail* prove that he is on solid, historically accurate ground? Does the work of Baigent, Leigh, and Lincoln open the possibility that there might actually be a bloodline in

European nobility that can be traced to a child of Jesus and Mary Magdalene?

It's strange ground to which Brown has led us, but two key questions will help us negotiate this territory:

1. What is the hypothesis presented in *Holy Blood, Holy Grail*?

2. Is *Holy Blood, Holy Grail* history or conspiracy theory?

These questions, though seemingly basic, lead us to a number of complex issues— from the issue of the historical authority of the gospels, which we have in part already discussed, to what can be counted as credible evidence in any endeavor of historical research. In any case, let us turn to those questions.

What Is the Hypothesis Presented in *Holy Blood, Holy Grail*?

According to Lincoln, Leigh, and Baigent, the evidence they encountered in their research led them to a hypothetical scenario in which Mary Magdalene was the wife of Jesus, with whom she produced offspring. Following the crucifixion, Mary and whatever children existed snuck into Gaul, where they would have found refuge in the Jewish communities existing there. The bloodline of Jesus was perpetuated by dynastic intermarriages between the Jewish families, Romans, and Visigoths. By the fifth century, Jesus' lineage became allied with the line of the Franks, producing the Merovingian dynasty.

According to this theory, the Merovingian dynasty was removed from power by a conspiracy between the Carolingian family and the Roman Catholic church, whose teachings obscure the truth about Jesus' life. Furthermore, according to this hypothesis, a secret society known as *The Priory of Sion* holds proof of the connection between Jesus and the Merovingian line. The Priory has supposedly been working behind the scenes to restore the bloodline to thrones in Europe to create a sort of "theocratic United States of Europe…assembled into a modern empire and ruled by a dynasty descended from Jesus" (*Holy Blood, Holy Grail*, 41). The three authors argue their case both on historical grounds and by providing evidence from the biblical text.

Historical Evidence

CLUE ONE: SECRET DOCUMENTS

According to *Holy Blood, Holy Grail*, in 1956 a series of books, documents, letters to the editor, and other sources of information began to emerge in France. Although the authors mention several of these documents, the most important to them were two collections of privately published documents known as *Dossiers Secrets* and *Le Serpent Rouge*.

Among the items found in the *Rouge* collection were a genealogy of the Merovingian dynasty, two maps of France during the Merovingian period, a ground plan of Paris' St. Sulpice Church, and thirteen short prose poems, each of which corresponded to a sign of the zodiac at that time. Of particular interest to the *Holy Blood* writers was one of these poems, with its reference to Mary Magdalene:

> To others, she is MAGDALENE, of the celebrated vase
> with the healing balm.
> The initiated know her true name: NOTRE DAME DES
> CROSS.

Notre Dame des Cross is generally a title designating the Virgin Mary, so this proved puzzling to Lincoln, Baigent, and Leigh. Even considering the fact that many French people maintain a strong tradition of devotion to Mary Magdalene, including a legend that she brought the Holy Grail to Gaul, it seemed strange to have a reference to Magdalene that associated her with maternity (*Notre Dame*).

Among the news clippings, letters, and pamphlets in *Dossiers Secrets* was a list of "Grand Masters" of a secret society known as the *Prieure' de Sion* (Priory of Sion). The list included such notable historical figures as Leonardo da Vinci, Isaac Newton, and Victor Hugo. What could connect these seemingly unrelated documents? And what was The Priory of Sion?

CLUE TWO: A SECRET SOCIETY

According to the *Holy Blood* team, The Priory of Sion could be traced to Godfroi de Bouillion, duke of Lorraine, who led the conquest of Jerusalem in 1099. The Priory functioned as a secret society working behind the scenes, supporting the Knights of the Templar, an order of monastic knights founded in 1139 to protect pilgrims traveling to Jerusalem. In 1139, the knights swore sole allegiance to Pope Innocent II and became a powerful force in diplomacy between nations. However, King Phillipe IV wished to bring the knights under his control, so the order was arrested and accused of a variety of things, from engaging in homosexual activity to ritually spitting on the cross and denying the resurrection. In 1312 a papal order dissolved the Knights Templar.

Lincoln, Leigh, and Baigent allege, however, that The Priory survived and orchestrated important events in Western history. In fact, these writers claim The Priory still plays an important clandestine role in international affairs. This clandestine influence, in fact, is wielded to meet a single objective: the restoration of the Merovingian bloodline and dynasty to France and other monarchies in Europe. Of course, this strange goal raises the question: Who were the Merovingians?

CLUE THREE: THE MEROVINGIANS

The Merovingian dynasty owes its name to Merovech, the leader of the Salian Franks from 447 to 456. According to the *Holy Blood* team, an ancient legend holds that Merovech had two fathers—his mother, while pregnant with him, went swimming and was raped by a sea-creature, impregnating her a second time. The legend maintains that the blood of both fathers therefore flowed through Merovech's veins.

Historically, the military victories of Chideric I against the Visigoths, Saxons, and Alamanni brought the dynasty into prominence, as did the consolidation of Gaul north of the Loire (486), the adoption of Roman Catholicism (496), and the decisive victory over the Visigoths (507), all actions of Childeric's son Clovis I.

However, in the early seventh century, the Merovingian kings began to allot more and more daily administration to the *major domo*, a palace mayor so to speak. This position soon became hereditary in the Carolingian family, who eventually deposed the Merovingians.

According to the *Holy Blood* writers, following Clovis's conversion to Catholicism, he made a secret pact with the church, the details of which are rather sketchy. However, Clovis' son, Dagobert II curbed the political expansion of church. He also married a Visigoth woman, an action that may have implied sympathy for Arian theology, since the writers suggest such theology still heavily influenced Visigoth Christianity. Dagobert was killed in a hunting accident in 679, which many (including the *Holy Blood* writers) assume to be the result of a conspiracy between the Roman Catholic church and *Major Domo* Pepen the Fat.

The Merovingian kings following Dagobert essentially were monarchs only in the nominal sense. In 732, an Arab army from Spain invaded France. Who led the French army that met and defeated the Arabs? The leader was not a Merovingian. Rather, the *Major Domo* Charles Martel won the French victory. Martel's heir, Pippin III, gathered support among Frankish nobles for a change in dynasty. When the Pope appealed to Pippin for military assistance, Pippin insisted that the church sanction his coronation in exchange. So in 751, Childeric II, the last Merovingian, was deposed. He was allowed to live, but his long hair was cut, and he was sent to a monastery. The reign of the Carolingian dynasty began.

According to Baigent, Leigh, and Lincoln, among the hidden documents they discovered was a genealogy that attached Godfroi de Bouillon, the crusader who led the conquest of Jerusalem, to the Merovingian line. Bouillon's conquest, as we have noted, came in 1099, three hundred years or so after Childeric was deposed. What might be relevant about these seemingly innocuous genealogical connections?

CLUE FOUR: THE HOLY GRAIL

During the Medieval period, literary pieces centering around the Holy Grail proliferated. They became known as "grail romances." Baigent, Leigh, and Lincoln examine several of these. They pay closest attention to Wolfram Von Eschenbach's, written around 1195–1216 C.E. In Von Eschenbach's opus, the Knights of the Templar serve as guardians of the grail family. The family seems to have incurred God's wrath at some point (which Baigent, Leigh, and Lincoln interpret as a possible allusion to Jewish roots), but have regained divine favor and power. However, they must intermarry to keep their lineage alive.

The *Holy Blood* team points out that most grail romances focus on King Arthur, whose name means "Bear," a symbol that often referred to the Merovingians. They therefore raise the question as to whether Arthurian legends might actually be appropriations of Merovingian stories.

Likewise, the team examines another word for the Holy Grail, *Sangraal.* They break this into two root words, *sang raal,* (or *sang royal*), which translates as royal blood. The grail was the cup used not only at the biblical Last Supper but also at the crucifixion to catch Christ's blood. It is always considered to be a receptacle of Jesus' blood, but the linguistic breakdown, according to Lincoln, Baigent, and Leigh, demonstrates that the grail is the receptacle of Jesus' *bloodline.*

Taking these three pieces of information, the team reasons that the Holy Grail literature is a coded collection that communicates the story of the endurance of Jesus' bloodline through the Merovingian dynasty.

CLUE FIVE: THE CHURCH

In *Holy Blood, Holy Grail's* hypothetical schema, the church emerges as a conspirator to maintain the secret of the existence of Jesus' bloodline. The writers hypothesize that the early Jesus movement comprised two main camps. One camp supported the creation of a family dynasty in which Jesus (traditionally revered as from the line of David) and Mary Magdalene (who according to some traditions was from the line of Benjamin) would have restored the Israelite monarchy. Another camp consisted of adherents to the message of Jesus' teachings. Following the crucifixion, the tradition that received the most mainstream support was that of Jesus' message. To win converts in the Roman empire, however, this message evolved from ethical and spiritual teachings into a syncretistic amalgam of Greco-Roman traditions.

According to this theory, as the Christian system evolved and the Roman church became more powerful, the church did everything possible to suppress the truth about Jesus, his human origins, aspirations to restore the monarchy, and the continuance of his bloodline. The church in this theory feared that the truth would upset the *mythos* on which the church's power rested. Hence, the church made the pact with Clovis to repress the truth of the Merovingian origins and played a role in the assassination of Dagobert, who wished to curb the expanding power of the church that had usurped power from Jesus' true heirs.

Despite the church's repression the truth lived on in legends such as the grail romances and the story of Merovech's origins. (The fish, after all, was an early symbol for Jesus and could explain the myth of the sea-creature's blood flowing through the Merovingian dynasty.)

Historical Conclusion

These clues therefore form the skeleton of a hypothesis about the marriage and bloodline of Jesus. However, as the authors point out, their historical analysis was not sufficient to prove their case. Therefore they turned to another source to substantiate their argument: The Bible.

Biblical Evidence

Clue One: The Credibility of Scripture

The very use of the Bible by the *Holy Blood* authors is intriguing in itself. They are incredibly skeptical of its use in substantiating any sort of historical hypothesis, calling the process by which the canon was formed "arbitrary." They are quick to point out the contradictions and discrepancies between the gospels, asserting that these contradictions, as well as the many editorial redactions evident in the comparison of manuscripts written in different periods of the church, shake the credibility of the gospels as historical sources.

Likewise, they emphasize that the gospels were heavily colored by a need to appeal to and placate Roman authority. This led to the scapegoating of the Jews for Jesus' death, further obscuring the true message of Jesus. Therefore, what value could any of the gospels have for their research?

CLUE TWO: THE AUTHORITY OF JOHN

Interestingly enough, despite what I understand to be the normative claim of most contemporary biblical scholarship (Robert Kysar gives a balanced presentation of the issues; see "For Further Reading" on page 76), the *Holy Blood* team claims that the gospel of John is the most historically authoritative gospel. They base this on their own research and what they claim to be the most prevalent assumption about the gospels in biblical scholarship.

They acknowledge John's late composition. Still, they argue, the fact that John recalls many stories that do not appear in the synoptics (including the Wedding at Cana, the role of Joseph of Arimithea, and the raising of Lazarus) may make it a more reliable source. After all, these stories were obviously not censored, as they might have been in the synoptics. Likewise, the gospel of John's focus on Jerusalem as a locus of Jesus' activity rather than on Galilee, as is the case in the synoptics, also leads them to believe that John may be a more reliable source.

CLUE THREE: THE WEDDING AT CANA

John 2:1–12 records the story of a wedding at Cana, where Jesus turned water into wine. According to Baigent, Leigh, and Lincoln, this passage may be a rendering of Jesus' own wedding, preserved in the gospel, though edited to obscure what actually happened.

The three writers reason that in terms of the culture of the period it would have been "glaringly conspicuous" if Jesus were not married, especially if he were a rabbi in the strictest sense of the word. The dominant scholarly perception of Jesus is that he was an itinerant teacher who had little to no formal training. The *Holy Blood* team raises the possibility that he may have had rabbinical training. If that were so, at least according to later Mishnaic tradition, he would have had to be married.

In terms of the wedding at Cana, the authors surmise that it would be highly unusual for two guests—Jesus and his mother—to be concerned with providing wine for the other guests. However, if Jesus were the groom, they reason, it would make sense for the two of them to be concerned.

Furthermore, they cite the reference to a bridegroom in 2:9–10 as a possible reference to Jesus. The words of the house steward—"Everyone serves the good wine first...but you have kept the good wine until now,"—according to the authors seem to be addressed toward Jesus, who would, in their scenario, be the bridegroom.

Clue Four: Political Importance of Jesus' Marriage

Though Baigent, Lincoln, and Leigh note that the wedding as presented in the gospel of John was a "modest local ceremony," they suggest that it might have actually been an "extravagant aristocratic union" serving an important political purpose. Although John makes no reference to Jesus' lineage, the gospels of Matthew and Luke both claim Jesus descended from the great Israelite king, David. A later tradition also holds that Mary Magdalene belonged to the tribe of Benjamin, from whom Saul, David's predecessor as leader of Israel, came. According to the *Holy Blood* writers, this wedding between Jesus and Mary could have been the first step toward insurrection:

> As far as we could see, it made sound political sense. Jesus would have been a priest-king of the line of David who possessed a legitimate claim to the throne. He would have consolidated his position by a symbolically important dynastic marriage. He would have then been poised to unify his country, mobilize the populace behind him, drive out the oppressors, and restore the glory of the monarchy as it was under Solomon.

According to the *Holy Blood* hypothesis, then, Jesus was preparing for the overthrow of Rome and a restoration of Jerusalem's glory. But before he was able to do so, he was captured and crucified.

Or was he?

CLUE FIVE: CRUCIFIXION AS A HOAX

Baigent, Leigh, and Lincoln note that their theory does not rest on the results of the crucifixion. Mary Magdalene and the heir of Jesus, they reason, could have been smuggled to a Jewish community in Gaul whether or not Jesus survived. However, they do present another hypothesis dealing with the crucifixion. This attempts to explain the resurrection appearances of Jesus without relying on the miraculous.

According to their account, the crucifixion was an elaborate hoax. They suggest that the wine (or vinegar) Jesus received (Jn. 19:29–30) was actually an opiate of some sort. The opiate's effects gave Jesus the appearance of death. Furthermore, crucifixion generally led to a slow death, unless the legs of the crucified were broken, hastening the victim's suffocation. Because Jesus seemed to die quickly, his legs were not broken (19:33). The biblical account contends that this was because he was already dead. According to the *Holy Blood, Holy Grail* account, the drugging of Jesus allowed him to appear dead, preventing him from having his legs broken and actually being killed.

This theory assigns an important role to Joseph of Arimithea. According to legend he was the keeper of the grail. John says Joseph was responsible for Jesus' burial, but the *Holy Blood* theory claims that Joseph plotted this hoax of Jesus' death with none other than Pontius Pilate (perhaps explaining the fact that Pilate is portrayed sympathetically in the gospels). This is in part based on a reference to the friendship of Pilate and Joseph in *The Gospel of Peter,* one of the non-canonical gospels we discussed previously.

Jesus was therefore able to escape crucifixion and regroup, making plans for his next move, at least according to the *Holy Blood, Holy Grail* theory.

CLUE SIX: LAZARUS

The final key in this alternate history is Lazarus. In the gospel of John, Lazarus is the brother of two women named Martha and Mary. After Lazarus died, Jesus raised him from the dead (Jn. 11). Though most scholars believe the Mary in this story is not Mary Magdalene, Baigent, Leigh, and Lincoln accept her as such, making Lazarus and Jesus brothers-in-law. Likewise, in their estimation, the resurrection of Lazarus was not an actual resurrection from the dead, but was instead a ritual of initiation that brought Lazarus into a symbolic death and rebirth (similar to the language surrounding rites of baptism).

Citing their familial relationship and the theories of at least one biblical scholar, the *Holy Blood* team suggests that the "beloved disciple" of John's gospel (Jn. 13:23; 20:2; 21:7, 20) is, in fact, Lazarus. At the end of John's gospel, Jesus says of the beloved disciple, "If it is my will that he remain until I come, what is that to you?" (21:22). The theory posits that this refers to future plans Jesus would need to make with the beloved disciple, possibly concerning the escape of Mary with the heir of Jesus to Gaul.

NEW TESTAMENT CONCLUSION

Baigent, Leigh, and Lincoln are able to weave an interpretation of the Fourth Gospel that supports their theory. By calling on characters such as Joseph of Arimithea, Lazarus, and Mary Magdalene, they are able to suggest a far more politically charged account of the life of Jesus than that to which we are accustomed to hearing. But is this alternative reading of history credible? Is it, in fact, history?

Is *Holy Blood, Holy Grail* History or Conspiracy Theory?

Holy Blood, Holy Grail is many things—a detailed synthesis of a variety of streams of information, an ambitious attempt to prove a hypothesis, and a best-selling shocker. Unfortunately, it is not history. I would argue that it is instead a product of what we might describe as conspiracy theory.

Essentially, the differences in historical inquiry and conspiracy theory are not only differences in method, but differences in orientation toward the use of information. In historical inquiry, as with most intellectual endeavors, hypotheses emerge from a gathering of information on historical incidents. The credibility of the hypothesis is then scrutinized based on the further study of these incidents, documentary evidence surrounding them, and the relationship of those incidents to prior, contemporary, or subsequent incidents. Based on the gathering of information, the hypothesis is accepted, tweaked, or discounted.

However, in conspiracy theory, hypotheses are not manufactured to be scrutinized. Rather, they are posited to be proven. When information contradicts a conspiracy theory-styled hypothesis, theorists do not tweak the hypothesis. Instead, they tweak the piece of information. When a piece of information conflicts with the hypothesis, a conspiracy theorist will often examine what that information might obscure rather than examining what it illuminates. For example, a piece of information that goes counter to a writer's hypothesis might be read as information disseminated by a powerful force to hide the truth. Truth in this view can only be reconstructed by historical detective work. This results in a hypothesis built on many mini-hypotheses—castles essentially, built of sand.

Additionally, in history, substantiating the factuality of information through comparing and scrutinizing multiple sources on a subject is a key component of proving a hypothesis. In conspiracy theory, however, the least accepted source or theory often seems to be the most credible. After all, to the conspiracy theorist, oft-repeated information has the least amount of credibility because it is disseminated so that the truth will be obscured. As a result, innuendo, legends, and highly subjective sources are often presented as completely—and indisputably—factual.

This is not to say that much of the information at the root of the theories presented in *Holy Blood, Holy Grail* is without merit. Likewise, some of the theories they appropriate in making their claim are well-accepted in mainstream scholarship. However, they often draw much wider conclusions from these theories and pieces of information than may be prudent. In terms of the biblical text, let's examine a few.

Biblical Evidence

Clue One: The Bible as Historical Authority

As the *Holy Blood* writers argue and as we have discussed in earlier chapters, many gospels did not make it into the biblical canon. The fact that these books did not make the cut does *not necessarily prove* that omission of these texts obscured historical facts. As we have discussed, theological claims were often the mitigating factors in the acceptability of a gospel to the Christian community.

Likewise, the discrepancies and varied viewpoints among the books of the Bible do not make either Testament an arbitrary collection, as the *Holy Blood* team claims. Rather, the Bible reflects a history of diverse opinions on the events of the Israelite and early Christian traditions. Scholars of the Bible are well aware of its discrepancies. However, this does not mean we can glean nothing historical from the synoptic gospels, for example, even if I have argued that they probably tell us more about first-century understandings of the implications of the life and ministry of Jesus than they tell us about the historical particulars of his life and ministry.

Clue Two: John vs. Synoptic Authority

Interestingly, the *Holy Blood* team asserts that John, not Mark, exhibits the most historical credibility. For Baigent, Leigh, and Lincoln, the existence of several traditions that do not appear in the synoptics raises the possibility that these traditions were repressed in the other gospels. For example, they use a recently discovered document known as "The Secret Gospel of Mark," to make their case. This document contains a short narrative about the resurrection of a young man somewhat parallel to the Lazarus narrative. The authenticity of "Secret Gospel" has long been disputed, and many scholars believe it to be a fraud. But the *Holy Blood* team nonetheless points to its parallel with the Lazarus story and its hypothetical suppression as proof that John was not tampered with as much as the synoptics. They claim that though John is estimated to have a later date, it is still more historically accurate than the synoptics. They also cite John as a fuller narrative, reading this as evidence that its writer was probably relying on more accurate eyewitness reports. Most scholars argue, however, that this is the result of a community that was more theologically advanced, more integrated into Greco-Roman intellectual life (as indicated by the adoption of the *logos* concept), and therefore, a later text that contained more theological extrapolation than the synoptics. For example, one finds in John long speeches of Jesus with no parallels in any other gospel—not because they were actual words suppressed by the church but because they were theological tractates that emerged out of Johannine teaching about Jesus.

The *Holy Blood* team also cites two scholars, S. G. F. Brandon and C. H. Dodd, who seem to support the supremacy of historicity in John. However, a closer look at the passages that Baigent, Leigh, and Lincoln quote reveals that this is not quite the case. In Dodd's book, *Historical Tradition in the Fourth Gospel*, he does argue that "Behind the Fourth Gospel lies an ancient tradition independent of the other Gospels." However, in suggesting that Dodd argues for the historical supremacy of John, the *Holy Blood* writers misrepresent this quote. Many of Dodd's contemporaries completely dismissed the possibility of John's having *any* historical value. In arguing that John did represent a historical tradition, he was arguing against assumptions that John's text was simply an extrapolation from the synoptics. It is perhaps fair to say that for Dodd, the Fourth Gospel was as valid a historical source as the synoptics, not a superior historical source. As a means of corroboration, the *Holy Blood* team cites Brandon as another scholar who holds this view, but a quick review of the text by Brandon reveals that he is quoting Dodd! The *Holy Blood, Holy Grail* writers are not producing independent, corroborating evidence at all. In fact, they are simply leading us in circles. Their argument for Johannine primacy falls flat.

CLUE THREE: THE CRUCIFIXION

Holy Blood, Holy Grail's hypothesis surrounding the crucifixion hoax is not a new theory. The Enlightenment intellectual period, stretching from approximately the seventeenth century to the beginning of the nineteenth, was renowned for a predilection for optimism and supreme trust in the power of reason. In this period theories abounded explaining the crucifixion in reasonable terms. In these Enlightenment-era theories, Jesus' disciples were hypothesized to have faked the resurrection by emptying out Jesus' tomb, as well as fooling the authorities with ploys similar to those championed by Baigent, Lincoln, and Leigh (compare Mt. 28:11–15). This reliance on finding a "reasonable," rational explanation for the crucifixion assumed that the gospels were written by superstitious—or dishonest—followers and that the miracles they recounted had a reasonable, natural explanation.

Such theories fit into a spectrum of historical explanations for what happened on the cross and in the tomb. Just this century, countless books have been written across this spectrum, touting everything from the historicity of a literal interpretation of the resurrection to theories such as that of John Dominic Crossan, who contended that part of the public shame of crucifixion was that following death the victims' bodies were not removed from crosses, but were actually consumed by wild animals.

Whether or not one believes any of the possible theories advanced by Jesus historians (a category to which I momentarily, though skeptically, place Baigent, Leigh, and Lincoln), the fact is, much of what makes their arguments convincing is not the historical evidence they put on display, but the rhetorical tools they use in displaying it. Baigent, Leigh, and Lincoln are masterful in their use of rhetoric. Turning phrases such as "a private crucifixion on private property leaves considerable room for a hoax," and "Jesus' death occurs at a moment that is almost too convenient, too felicitously opportune" adds rhetorical strength to their argument, sensationalizing whatever facts they have, and obscuring the evidence that they lack.

Historical Evidence

Clue One: "Synthesis"

According to the *Holy Blood* writers, conventional methods of historical analysis were not sufficient for their research. Therefore, they argued that their work needed an interdisciplinary approach that synthesized a variety of methods of inquiry. The examination of biblical texts certainly benefits from the contributions of a variety of intellectual traditions, including literary studies, the social sciences, history, archeology, and many others. Still, the authors' claim to use an "interdisciplinary approach" helps them to obscure the fact that their use of disciplines is as "felicitously opportune" as the events they hypothesize.

Clue Two: Reading Legends as Maps

Another key issue in the synthesis offered by the *Holy Blood* team is its use of literary sources, especially the medieval grail romances. As is the case with most of the evidence they examine, Baigent, Leigh, and Lincoln only examine interpretations of these legends that favor their theory. As with most allegorical literary forms, the interpretations they favor are heavily contested, and certainly not definitive.

Because the interpretation of literature is a contentious enterprise, it is not only difficult to assume that a single interpretation is definitive; it is also difficult to extrapolate a historical record from a literary text. The contention that the repercussions of facts can be read through myths and legends contains a certain amount of truth, but reading correctly in this way is a tricky endeavor. Legends and myths may contain the residuals of historical evidence, but those residuals are mediated by other elements—often purely literary—that can be easily confused with one another if one assumes that literary legends lead to historical antecedents.

Clue Three: Evidence vs. Innuendo

The rhetorical style of the *Holy Blood* writers allows them to easily present innuendo and highly disputed findings as evidence and proven facts. For example, the writers recount their experiences in reading the *Le Serpents Rouge* and *Dossiers*

Secrets and in connecting those two documents to local rumor and innuendo about The Priory of Sion (including recounting a dead-end search for a headquarters as proof of The Priory's secrecy and ability to use influence to remain covert). Leigh, Baigent, and Lincoln then insist that their evidence substantiates "indisputable facts" connecting The Priory, the Knights Templar, and the Merovingian dynasty. Unfortunately, the validity of these facts is highly questionable, as the evidence was often drawn from the documentary intimations of a singular source: The Priory of Sion itself.

CLUE FOUR: FACTS IN THE WAY

In the February 22, 2004, edition of *The New York Times Review of Books*, Laura Miller writes in her essay, "The Da Vinci Con," about the legitimacy of the *Holy Blood, Holy Grail* hypothesis. She notes that Baigent, Leigh, and Lincoln suggest that the documents they found supporting the existence of The Priory were planted there by Pierre Plantard, who essentially manufactured all the evidence linking the Merovingians, grail legends, and The Priory of Sion. According to evidence readily available in a number of French books or by a quick Internet search, Miller contends, Plantard was not a source to be trusted:

> Plantard, it eventually came out, was an inveterate rascal with a criminal record for fraud and affiliations with wartime anti-Semitic and right-wing groups. The actual Priory of Sion was a tiny, harmless group of like-minded friends formed in 1956.

Essentially, the clamor created by *Holy Blood, Holy Grail* did not lead to a revolution in how the Christian faith is perceived, as its authors implied it could, but instead deflated easily, dismissed by those vigilant enough to check the authenticity of the *Holy Blood* hypothesis.

Conclusion: The Story behind the Story

Through a complex array of intellectual twists and turns, *Holy Blood, Holy Grail* presents an intriguing theory about the life of Jesus. By using questionable sources and relying on a methodology that meshes disciplines somewhat unevenly together, its authors push for the credibility of a theory concerning the bloodline of Jesus. Regardless of the legitimacy of this theory, it serves as the intellectual basis for *The Da Vinci Code*. In *The Da Vinci Code*, Dan Brown weaves a narrative around the *Holy Blood, Holy Grail* theory that has captivated countless readers. Not only has the story of a truth hidden and suppressed by the church proven to be an exciting mystery, but it has also inspired readers to search the apocryphal gospels and the roots of Christian history, hoping to find answers that will lead to the truth they believe the church has hidden.

But has the church hidden truths and facts about the life of Jesus? Even if the *Holy Blood, Holy Grail* hypothesis is filled with problems, does it still point to the possibility that long-hidden articles exist that the church would do anything to keep secret? Does an organization like *Opus Dei* exist to protect an ancient deception? It is to that possibility we now turn.

DISCUSSION QUESTIONS

1. Do the writers of *Holy Blood, Holy Grail* present a plausible hypothesis? Why or why not? What is most convincing about their argument?

2. Should Dan Brown present the existence of The Priory of Sion as a historical fact? Why or why not?

3. Do you think one of the gospels is more historically accurate than the others? Which one, and why?

For Further Reading

Baigent, Michael, Richard Leigh, and Henry Lincoln. *Holy Blood, Holy Grail*. New York: Dell, 1983.

Brandon, S. G. F. *Jesus and the Zealots*. Manchester: Manchester Univ. Press, 1967.

Dodd, C. H. *Historical Tradition in the Fourth Gospel.* Cambridge, Eng.: Cambridge Univ. Press, 1963.

Kysar, Robert. "John, the Gospel of." In *The Anchor Bible Dictionary.* New York: Doubleday, 1992.

Miller, Laura. "The Da Vinci Con." *The New York Times Book Review,* 22 February 2004, p. 23.

CHAPTER 5

Has the Church Conspired to Repress the Truth about Jesus?

"Many call Opus Dei a brainwashing cult," reporters often challenged. "Others call you an ultraconservative Christian secret society. Which are you?"

"Opus Dei is neither," the bishop would patiently reply. "We are a Catholic Church. We are a congregation of Catholics who have chosen as our priority to follow Catholic doctrine as rigorously as we can in our own daily lives."

(*The Da Vinci Code*, 29)

We also want to point out that The Da Vinci Code's *bizarre depiction of Opus Dei is inaccurate, both in the overall impression and in many details, and it would be irresponsible to form any opinion of Opus Dei based on reading* The Da Vinci Code.

(from www.opusdei.org)

Since many have undertaken to set down an orderly account of the events that have been fulfilled among us, just as they were handed on to us by those who from the beginning were eyewitnesses and servants of the word, I too decided, after investigating everything carefully from the very first, to write an orderly account for you, most excellent, Theophilus, so that you might know the truth concerning the things about which you have been instructed.

(Lk. 1:1–4)

The Priory of Sion is not the only group around which Dan Brown weaves a sense of intrigue. Some of the most sinister behavior he describes in the novel is done in the name of a special prelature of the Roman Catholic Church known as *Opus Dei*. On the same "Facts" page that describes The Priory, Brown describes Opus Dei in the following way:

The Vatican prelature known as Opus Dei is a deeply devout Catholic sect that has been the topic of recent controversy due to reports of brain-washing, coercion, and a dangerous practice known as "corporal mortification." Opus Dei has just completed construction of a $47 million National Headquarters at 243 Lexington Avenue in New York City.

This statement is true. Yes, accusations of cultlike behavior have been lodged concerning Opus Dei. They have acquired property that raises questions about their access to financial resources and top-secret bookkeeping. Still, Brown's statement does not tell the whole story about this controversial group. In fact, his characterization of Opus Dei has been a source of controversy itself.

Brown presents two characters related intimately to Opus Dei: The desperate, power-hungry Bishop Aringarosa and the albino monk Silas. According to Brown's story, a newly appointed Pope revokes the special status of Opus Dei. Aringarosa, desperate to cling to his power and authority, becomes involved in a nefarious plot with an anonymous patron known only as "the Teacher." They seek to blackmail the Vatican with the "truth" about the bloodline of Jesus. They then enlist Silas, the albino numerary of Opus Dei whom Aringarosa had taken under his wing, to do the "dirty work" of retrieving the grail.

A couple of issues arise from this section of the plot. First, it assumes that the hierarchy of the church has deceived church followers for centuries by concealing facts about the life of Jesus. Second, it assumes that revealing the truth about the life of Jesus would damage the church's power and prestige and that the church would do anything to maintain those secrets. According to Teabing, who is revealed to be the Teacher, "The Church may no longer employ crusaders to slaughter non-believers, but their influence is no less persuasive. No less insidious" (*The Da Vinci Code*, 407). Third, it implies that the financial contributions of Opus Dei sustain its favored position in the church and that what it demands from its members is merely tolerated, not supported, by the greater church.

These assumptions lead us to three questions to investigate:

1. What is *Opus Dei*, and what is its purpose?
2. Is the church threatened by research on the life of Jesus?
3. Can we know the truth about the life of Jesus?

In answering these questions, we will investigate the history of Opus Dei, its critics' descriptions of its practices, its stance on *The Da Vinci Code*, and how it might fit into the larger question of what constitutes truth in a religious tradition. We will also look briefly at the purported "threat" that the truth about the life of Jesus might pose to the church's authority. Finally, we will look at a brief historical-critical take on what was once a widely accepted theological notion— the Virgin Birth—and what sort of implications that might have about how we understand the life of Jesus.

What Is Opus Dei and What Is Its Purpose?

CLUE ONE: THE HISTORY OF OPUS DEI

Opus Dei was founded in 1928 in Spain by Josemaria Escriva, a priest often referred to as "The Founder" or "The Father" by Opus Dei members. After receiving a divine vision, Escriva believed that God had charged him to build an organization that emphasized the spiritual lives and practices of Catholic laity. The name "Opus Dei" or "Work of God" emerged in the 1930s. It originally began as a movement exclusively for men. Following another divine revelation to Escriva, women were allowed to join in the 1930s, though separate branches were established for each gender. In 1936, the violence of the Spanish Civil War forced Escriva into hiding. Immediately after his return, he set up Opus Dei residential centers and academies, which attracted many recruits.

In 1943, the establishment of the Priestly Society of the Holy Cross allowed diocesan secular priests to join with Opus Dei in its activities without becoming part of its prelature. By the 1950s, Pope Pius XII had given definitive approval to Opus Dei, bolstering its position in Catholicism and attracting even more recruits.

Escriva died in 1976. At the time of his death, approximately sixty thousand people belonged to Opus Dei. Following his death, Opus Dei supporters began to campaign aggressively for Escriva to be canonized as a saint, a movement Opus Dei critics have vigorously resisted. In 1982, Pope John Paul II established Opus Dei as a personal prelature, giving its leader sole authority over its activities around the globe and freeing the organization from the supervision of bishops. Opus Dei is the only lay organization of the Catholic Church to have this status. It operates in more than sixty countries and counts a membership of at least eighty thousand, including two thousand priests.

CLUE TWO: PRACTICES AND CRITICS

According to the promotional material of Opus Dei, the organization's mission consists of the following:

> Opus Dei, with its essentially secular spirit, serves the Church and society by fostering individual holiness and apostolic commitment among the Christian faithful, helping them to discover and take on the demands of their baptismal vocation in the specific place they occupy in the world. (from www.opusdei.org)

In pursuing this mission, followers engage in a number of practices, including a weekly group meeting to discuss their participation in the movement, regular confession to a priest affiliated with Opus Dei, and discussion with their Opus Dei director on spiritual matters. Practices include a number of spiritual disciplines, among them a strict schedule of daily prayer, spiritual readings, and self-mortification.

According to many sources, self-mortification for Opus Dei members involves periodic fasting, self-flagellation, and the wearing of a spiked leg band called a cicile. *The Da Vinci Code* prominently features the cicile. Not surprisingly, self-mortification is one of the most controversial practices of the movement. Some residuals of self-mortification are still common in church practices, such as fasting and/or abstaining from meat during Lent. However, for the most part, self-mortification has disappeared from mainstream church practice. Likewise, Opus Dei has described the description of self-mortification in *The Da Vinci Code* as a "distorted and exaggerated depiction," although the statement does not directly address the issue of whether or not the practices described in the novel have any factual basis.

Beyond the issue of self-mortification, critics charge that other practices, including aggressive recruiting of impressionable young people, alienation from friends and family members who do not belong to Opus Dei, and sharp control over the finances and behavior of many members, are unhealthy and dangerous. In fact, many critics do not shy away from describing Opus Dei as a sect or cult, though its official status within the Catholic Church certainly makes such an accusation difficult to prove. Nonetheless, the Opus Dei goals of integrating spiritual discipline into the everyday lives of laity is often perceived as stringent enough to raise the concerns of many liberal Catholics and former Opus Dei members.

CLUE THREE: OPUS DEI ON *THE DA VINCI CODE*

As one might expect, Opus Dei has been quite critical of Dan Brown's depiction of the organization in *The Da Vinci Code*. In a statement available on their Web site, www.opusdei.org, they refute Brown's descriptions of their attitudes toward modernity and the reforms of Vatican II, the role of women in Opus Dei and in the Catholic Church, the self-mortification issue, the abuse of wealth and power by Opus Dei, and its apparent sectarian nature.

Opus Dei also sent a letter to Doubleday, *The Da Vinci Code*'s publisher, asking that they remove the introductory "FACT" page and edit some of the claims about the organization. Brown stuck by his story, insisting that his evidence was thoroughly researched. However, even critics of Opus Dei consider Brown's book to be a considerable exaggeration in its claims of manipulation and of greed for wealth and power being at the heart of the organization. Still, most of these critics do maintain their claims about practices of self-mortification and the overall rejection of the contemporary world within the organization.

Conclusion

Although most critics of Opus Dei consider it to be a tightly controlled, often unhealthy influence on its members, they are nonetheless skeptical of Brown's fictionalized account of an organization so driven by power that its leader would conspire to blackmail or overthrow the church. That leads us to another issue. Is there evidence about the life of Jesus that would make such a scheme possible?

Is the Church Threatened by Research on the Life of Jesus?

Not only is the pact between Teabing and Opus Dei forged out of Bishop Aringarosa's need to maintain his power and influence, but the element of blackmail involved relies on the assertion that the power of the church hinges on the truth about Jesus' life remaining secret. In fact, according to the novel, the death of Sophie's parents is suspected of being the work of the church. But does the church really fear that research on the life of Jesus will expose a 2000-year-old fraud?

Again we are drifting into the realm of conspiracy theory. I seriously doubt that the church is maintaining a secret hoax for the sake of its own power. Still, many people's suspicions are aroused by such a theory. Why? Because the hierarchy of the Catholic Church has sufficient historical precedent in resisting modernity and contemporary life. Even without considering the *Holy Blood, Holy Grail* theory and its fictionalized equivalent in *The Da Vinci Code*, does this mean that historical insight about the life of Jesus is threatening to the church? To answer such a question, we should turn to a quick history lesson.

CLUE ONE: THE CATHOLIC CHURCH FACES MODERNITY

Academic trends of the nineteenth century, most notably Darwin's *The Origin of Species* and historical-critical biblical criticism, often threatened deeply rooted Protestant and Catholic teachings. As some Catholic biblical scholars began to embrace historical-critical methods, the hierarchy of the church resisted. In 1907, Pope Pius X prepared a catalog of errors entitled *Lamentabili Sane Exitu.* It condemned sixty-five modernist "errors" concerning study of the Bible and called for an end to historical-critical analysis of the Bible. Some of the "errors" condemned in the catalog include the following:

> 11. Divine inspiration does not so extend to the whole Sacred Scripture so that it renders its parts, all and single, immune from all error.

> 35. Christ had not always the consciousness of His Messianic dignity.

> 52. It was foreign to the mind of Christ to found a Church as a Society which was to last on the earth for a long course of centuries; nay in the mind of Christ the Kingdom of Heaven together with the end of the world was about to come immediately.

Pius X also issued an encyclical letter entitled *Pascendi Dominici Gregis.* This condemned modernist thought as a corrupt monolith, accusing modernist thinkers of heresy. In 1910, the church required an anti-modernist oath of all priests. However, the modernist position did not simply fade away. With the Vatican II council, called by Pope John XXIII in 1962, the church became more open to many of the concerns of Catholic scholars who had modernist leanings or sympathies. Now, more than forty years after Vatican II, the insights of historical-critical biblical scholarship, though heavily debated within all church circles, are part of the intellectual tools used by Catholic and Protestant biblical scholars alike.

CLUE TWO: FAITH AND TRUTH

It is important that we not jump to too many conclusions in terms of the resistance of the Catholic Church to the use of biblical scholarship in the late nineteenth and early twentieth century. First, we should realize that it was not a struggle of Dogma versus Truth. It was a struggle between two fundamentally different perspectives on reality and what counts as truth. For the Catholic Church, the historical-critical method challenged basic assumptions about what is true about the life of Jesus and who we are as human beings. For adherents of the historical-critical method, Catholic doctrines impeded the dissemination of their historical research—which they considered to be objectively factual, and thereby true—to laity. Doctrine, of course, has its historical and human origins, and historical research, of course, is limited in its ability to demonstrate how facts can lead to objective, definitive truth.

Second, it is important to realize that this is not simply an issue that faces the Catholic Church. The repercussions of biblical criticism are still sources of controversy in some Protestant churches, from mainline to fundamentalist persuasions. The insights gained from this type of research often challenge things held as core parts of the Christian faith. Naturally these are difficult for many churchgoers to accept. If an individual's faith is dependent on the factual and historical infallibility of the Bible, the discovery that a long-held Christian tradition is historically problematic can be crushing. However, in many modern churches, Catholic and Protestant, contemporary biblical criticism informs Christian education and the preaching of biblical texts.

Conclusion

We must not frame this as an issue that creates an opposition of stereotypes: the outdated, oppressive Catholic Church and the progressive, embattled academy. In truth, ecclesial circles often exhibit as much progressive thinking as does the academic community. On the other hand, scholarly institutions show as much resistance to new insight as does the church.

That being said, do scholarly endeavors tell us anything about the life of Jesus? Even if they do not reveal that he had a wife and heir, can they tell us anything?

Can We Know the Truth about the Life of Jesus?

CLUE ONE: THE QUEST(S) FOR THE HISTORICAL JESUS

To talk about the historical Jesus is to presuppose a very important thing: The Jesus presented in the gospels cannot be equated automatically with the human being Jesus whose life is the basis for those presentations. To differentiate between the two does not necessarily mean that one assumes the presentation of Jesus in the gospels is in some way dishonest. It does mean that one assumes that interpretive layers have been added to the accounts of the life of Jesus, that details and ideas may have been added to explain the influence his life and ministry had on early Christian communities, for example. The first "quest" for the historical Jesus lasted from the end of the Enlightenment to the beginning of the twentieth century. This has led scholars to believe that they can discover a core—the Historical Jesus—by unraveling the interpretive layers that tradition and doctrine have added.

Albert Schweitzer's *The Quest of the Historical Jesus* essentially ended the first quest. He argues that rather than discovering a core, Jesus historians ended up adding their own interpretive layers, turning Jesus into someone who fit their own ideals. Ironically, critics can argue that Schweitzer, in insisting on an apocalyptic core to the teachings of Jesus, followed suit with those he criticized. In like fashion, critics have contended that the second quest, which lasted from the

1950s to the 1970s, often resulted in a Jesus in tune with the dominant intellectual trends of the period.

The third quest is now at hand and has often received the same sort of criticism. As scholars categorize Jesus as an itinerant Cynic philosopher, an eschatological prophet, an agent of justice and social change, or as a self-proclaimed Messiah, other scholars insist that such research does not uncover anything about the core of the life of Jesus. It simply adds the particular scholar's theological declarations or literary spins to the life of Jesus.

This is not to say that nothing can be gained from historical biblical criticism. Nor is it to say that historical critics just make things up. Rather, to venture on a quest for the historical Jesus is not only an arduous task, but it often seems a nearly impossible one. Apart from the Bible, virtually no historical evidence for the life of Jesus exists. The Pauline letters—the earliest accounts from the Bible—feature no details about Jesus' teachings or life, but are focused almost exclusively on the meaning of Jesus' death on the cross. Probably the best we can uncover through historical biblical criticism is evidence of what the early church thought about and knew of Jesus rather than a historical core that reveals an authentic, definitive, historical Jesus.

Clue Two: The Virgin Birth

To understand the contributions and problems raised by biblical criticism, we will look at one example from the life of Jesus. This has to do with the understanding that Mary was a virgin when Jesus was born, as recorded in Matthew 1:18–25 and Luke 1:26–38. The Matthean tradition specifically quotes Isaiah 7:14 as a prophecy predicting that Jesus would be born of a virgin:

> "Look, the virgin shall conceive and bear a son,
>   and they shall name him Emmanuel." (Mt. 1:23a)

If we take a closer look at the historical context in which the Isaiah text was written, as well as the historical circumstances surrounding the appropriation of the text in Matthew, we discover something a bit unexpected. First, if we read the entire text of Isaiah 7:1—8:18, we discover that this is not a passage predicting the birth of a messiah in generations to follow. According to chapter 7, Isaiah's prophecy addresses a particular historical incident:

> In the days of Ahaz son of Jotham son of Uzziah, king of Judah, King Rezin of Aram and King Pekah son of Remaliah of Israel went up to attack Jerusalem, but could not mount an attack against it. (Isa. 7:1)

Essentially, Pekah, the king of Israel, had joined forces with Rezin to form an alliance against the imminent invasion of the Assyrians. When Ahaz refused to join their alliance, they threatened to invade Judah and oust him in favor of someone who would join their alliance. At the behest of YHWH, Isaiah presents an oracle of three children with symbolic names—Shear-jashub (Isaiah's young son, whose name means "A remnant shall return"), Immanuel ("God is with us"), and Maher-shalal-hash-baz ("The spoil speeds, the prey hastens")—to convince Ahaz to stand fast and not join the alliance. However, Ahaz chooses to side with the Assyrians, resulting in Judah's becoming a vassal state while Israel is conquered.

When we read the passage in its entirety, we see that the birth of Immanuel is contextualized within the story of the Syro-Ephraimite war and refers to an event that will affect Judah and Israel in Ahaz's lifetime. It was not until the early days of Christianity, when Jesus' followers scoured the Septuagint to find references that might fit their experience of God in the ministry of Jesus, that this became associated with a messianic prophecy.

The Septuagint, as we briefly discussed in chapter 1, was a Greek translation of the Hebrew Scriptures. In Hebrew versions of Isaiah 7:14, the word referring to the mother of Immanuel is "*'almah*," generally translated to mean a young woman, with no reference to her sexual activity. Generally, in the Hebrew Bible, the word "*bethulah*" refers to a virgin (Gen. 24:16; Ex. 22:16; Lev. 21:3, 14). However, in the Septuagint, "*'almah*" was translated in Isaiah 7:14 as "*parthenos*," the Greek for virgin. Therefore, the first

Christians, who would have read Greek, not Hebrew, would have read the passage as the account of a virgin who would conceive, whereas the Hebrew would have read much differently:

> Therefore, the Lord himself will give you a sign. Look, the young woman is with child and shall bear a son, and shall name him Immanuel. (Isa. 7:14)

For the early Christians, who sought proof of the divinity and messiahship of Jesus, the Greek version of this passage became one of their cornerstone proof texts. A claim about Jesus being born to a virgin fit well into the Greco-Roman culture, which was filled with miraculous birth stories of famous heroes, both mythological and historical. These included Heracles, Alexander the Great, and Caesar Augustus. The proof text served as an excellent apologetic for a religious movement that depended on winning converts to grow.

Our historical-critical examination has shown us that Isaiah 7:14, while traditionally tied to the narrative of Jesus' life as a prophecy of his birth, was not written as a prophecy about the life of Jesus, but as a prophecy that was to be fulfilled during the life of Ahaz. Although such a brief examination does not definitively answer the question about how the virgin birth tradition arose, or why it exists in Luke, which does not depend on Isaiah 7 in the same way that Matthew does, it does demonstrate that there is a difference in the theological claims that the church has made about Jesus since its origins and what historical and textual evidence reveals or implies.

Clue Three: Interpretive Options

Does the historical-critical insight into the relationship between Isaiah 7 and Matthew 1 undo the authority of the Bible? Does it reveal that there are things the church wants to hide, including proof that it manipulated texts to justify Jesus' divinity?

That's certainly one way to look at the situation. However, we must also practice historical criticism on ourselves. As contemporary readers, we have a particular way of understanding how we read texts and how we analyze them in relation to their historical contexts. Our method is quite different from the point of view of first-century Christians. The interpretation of texts, the understanding of what history is, and the explanation of how texts reveal truth were all quite different. The use of Isaiah as a proof text was not a dishonest representation, but a fairly standard interpretive practice in which God was understood to speak freshly out of old texts. Many Christian communities still share such a belief. Of course, this holds in differing degrees. Some communities find proof in the Bible for current events such as wars and assassinations, while others see their hopes for social justice resonating in the hopes of the prophets.

Essentially, as individuals and as members of religious communities, we have the ability to make interpretive choices based on a variety of sources of authority, including church doctrine, tradition, the expectations of our communities, personal experience, and many other factors. Historical-critical research is only one of the many sources of insight that help determine what a sacred text means in a community and how that meaning influences the faith of that community. One of the interesting results to arise from the publication of *The Da Vinci Code* has been a new set of questions about what makes these influences viable and even about the influence of a text like *The Da Vinci Code* in communities of faith.

Conclusion

The role of an organization such as Opus Dei in the Catholic church, though highly questionable, and possibly problematic, does not match the insidiousness that Brown implicates in *The Da Vinci Code*. Opus Dei is a conservative—and potentially manipulative, as many critics note—force in the church, but not one that would threaten to completely undo the church's doctrinal structure for the sake of maintaining its own place in the hierarchical pecking order.

Likewise, much of what was once threatening about historical research of the Bible and early Christian history has been integrated into mainstream Protestant and Catholic scholarship. It has become one of the many influences on how Christians perceive their own traditions and faith. Such critical study done for the church can give great insight into the historical development of Christian beliefs, though Christian communities still have the task of interpreting how those insights might affect their understandings of what the life of Jesus means for their faith.

But in terms of *The Da Vinci Code*, how do we go about doing that? How do we integrate that book, a work of fiction, and all the historical clues we have investigated into how we think about our faith? The options are manifold. In the next chapter, I offer one of my own.

DISCUSSION QUESTIONS

1. How would you describe Opus Dei? Is it a church? How do you feel about its practices?

2. Dan Brown seems to take a lot of liberty with what he considers to be factual. On the other hand, *The Da Vinci Code* is a novel. What are his responsibilities in terms of how he represents facts, ideas, and events?

3. Do you think we gain insight into our faith through historical research and critical analysis of the Bible? Why or why not?

For Further Reading

Frick, Frank. *A Journey Through the Hebrew Scriptures.* Fort Worth, Tex.: Harcourt Brace, 1995.

Livingston, James. *Modern Christian Thought,* vol 1. Upper Saddle River, N.J.: Prentice Hall, 1997.

Schweitzer, Albert. *The Quest of the Historical Jesus.* New York: Macmillan, 1962.

Witherington, Ben III. *The Jesus Quest.* Downers Grove, Ill.: InterVarsity Press, 1995.

Web Sites for Further Information

"Opus Dei" at The New Religious Movements Web site at
the University of Virginia: http://religiousmovements.
lib.virginia.edu/nrms/dei.html#9

The Official Opus Dei Web site: http://www.opusdei.org

The Opus Dei Awareness Network (A Watchdog Group):
http://www.odan.org

CHAPTER 6

How Do These Two Stories Interact?

> *Langdon smiled. "Sophie, every faith in the world is based on fabrication. That is the definition of faith— acceptance of that which we imagine to be true, that which we cannot prove. Every religion describes God through metaphor, allegory, and exaggeration, from the early Egyptians through modern Sunday school. Metaphors are a way to help our minds process the unprocessible. The problems arise when we begin to believe literally in our own metaphors."*
>
> (*The Da Vinci Code*, 341–42)

> *We also constantly give thanks to God for this, that when you received the word of God that you heard from us, you accepted it not as a human word but as what it really is, God's word, which is also at work in you believers.*
>
> (1 Thess. 2:13)

For many of its readers, *The Da Vinci Code* has become more than an exciting mystery novel. Hidden church secrets, gospels that were unread for centuries, and whispers of conspiracy and murder, though fictionalized, have been enough to raise serious questions in the minds of many about the "truth" of their faith.

Throughout the first five chapters, I have examined many of the historical circumstances surrounding the issues raised in *The Da Vinci Code*, including the process by which the Bible was created, the divinity of Jesus, the role of Mary Magdalene in the early church, the hypothesis that an existing bloodline can be traced back to Jesus and Mary, and whether or not the church conspired to keep the truth about Jesus hidden from believers. I realize that even my discussion of these issues has the potential to "push people's buttons," so to speak. For example, even the hypothetical book "Q," a pretty rudimentary topic among biblical scholars and seminary students, might seem to be a startling, even heretical, concept to many readers. For many Christians, the idea that the history of the church can give rise to alternative readings such as *The Da Vinci Code*'s (regardless of the sketchiness of its historicity) forces them to review many of the basics of their faith. Even if the underlying story of *The Da Vinci Code*— that Jesus' bloodline exists today—proves highly questionable, what about the larger issue? Do a long history of theological contentions, religious syncretism involving Greco-Roman and other traditions, and suppressed alternative writings leave Christians with a faith that is little more than a mishmash of other traditions? Does the Christian story record an original experience of God in the world, or is it merely a parasitic narrative that drew on whatever influences it encountered? Is there anything historical about the Bible, or is it all myth and metaphor?

I turn to those issues in this chapter. In doing so, I examine the practice of Christianity in a particular way—*as the creation and transmission of a story about the nature of God within a community.* I therefore ask three central questions:

1. How does Christianity operate as a story in a community?

2. What value do unorthodox readings of the Christian story have in Christian communities?

3. What do we do with the Christian story after *The Da Vinci Code*?

How Does Christianity Operate as a Story?

CLUE ONE: READING AND LIVING

To call Christianity a story is not to dismiss it as a fairy tale. Instead, it is to affirm the power it has in helping us shape the way we see the world. All too often, in an age in which we obsess over facts and figures and believe that truth is revealed by statistical evidence and the fiscal bottom line, we dismiss the truth we encounter in the stories we tell one another. Although we may think that there is something escapist about finding truth in the myths and stories that come from our religious traditions, the fact is that they can communicate a type of truth often missed by a world obsessed with graphs, charts, and hard "facts."

According to the synoptic gospels, Jesus used parables to describe what the reign of God was like. We understand that these stories made surprising, often radical points, using recognizable contexts and everyday situations. However, we should also consider the way that the telling of a story shapes the ethical point of view of the community that encounters it. As David James Duncan, a professor of creative writing at the University of Montana writes in a 2003 issue of *Orion* magazine, what makes stories powerful is that they make us take seriously the Christian call to love our neighbors as ourselves:

> The attempt to *imagine* thy neighbor as thyself is the daily work of every literary writer and reader I know. Literature's sometimes troubling, sometimes hilarious depictions of those annoying buffoons, our neighbors, may be the greatest gift we writers give the world when they become warm-up exercises for the leap toward actually *loving* them. Ernest Hemingway made a wonderful statement about this. "Make it up so truly," he advised, "that later it will happen that way." This is, I dare say, Christ-like advice, not just to those practicing an art form known

as fiction writing, but to anyone trying to live a faith, defend the weak, or love a neighbor.

The telling of stories is integral to who we are as human beings. While the last two thousand years of Christianity have produced complex theological doctrines, moral laws, and philosophical traditions, at the root of all of these things is a powerful story. For me, despite the many complex historical issues that surround it—issues that should not be ignored—the Christian story remains a story about a God who loves humanity and a human being whose life communicated that love.

CLUE TWO: SYMBIOSIS

Symbiosis, a term from the biological sciences, refers to two dissimilar organisms living together in a mutually advantageous relationship. When I describe a community and story as having a symbiotic relationship, I am asserting that the reading of a story in a community helps to give shape to the ethics, practices, and thinking of that community; likewise, as communities engage these stories, they are active in interpreting them according to the experiences (both historical and contemporary) of the community and its individual members.

The beliefs that make us who we are as a community of faith are not simply based on the Christian story, therefore, but on how we, as individuals and a community, read and interpret that story. Of course, how we understand the Christian story arises out of a number of things—our life experiences, the type of teaching about the faith to which we are exposed, the community's standards on the authority of scripture, the authority of leaders in the community in establishing interpretive norms, and outside cultural influences. All these things set a community's parameters on how the Christian story might be interpreted. Likewise, because new influences are always arising, these parameters are constantly changing and evolving—sometimes expanding, but often retracting, depending on the interaction of a community with a variety of influences.

As more and more people of faith read *The Da Vinci Code*, the role of the novel in this dynamic becomes an intriguing issue. For many people it becomes an alternative reading of the Christian story that does not meet the life experiences or standards of scriptural authority for their communities of faith. For others, it becomes one of the cultural influences that color how people of faith read the Bible. Nonetheless, *The Da Vinci Code* enters into the dynamic between a community and the stories it receives and tells. It becomes part of a community in which it is read, whether as a threat to what is long established or as a new influence woven into the fabric of the community's always developing interpretation of the Christian story.

Conclusion

We are a storytelling people. Much of the wisdom we have as human beings and as people of faith is communicated through story. To call Christianity a story is not to disregard its authority, influence, or legitimacy. Instead, it is to describe the way it weaves its way into our lives and becomes part of the way we understand what it means to be human. Likewise, the way we tell this story is influenced by a variety of other events, stories, and phenomena we encounter throughout the course of our lives. *The Da Vinci Code* is simply one more influential element. Our task is to make a conscious decision as to how the *Code* will influence our telling of the story.

What Is the Value of Unorthodox Readings of the Christian Story?

CLUE ONE: WHICH TEXTS ARE SACRED?

Early on, we examined Dan Brown's claim that the non-canonical gospels are the repositories of truth about the historical life of Jesus. We discovered that we have no evidence to substantiate such a claim and plenty of evidence to refute it. Still, we are left with another question—do these texts have anything to offer us as contemporary Christian communities? They've been lost to us for centuries, and they were once deemed either irrelevant or dangerous to the story of the church. Discovered anew, do they have value for us today? If so, what kind of value?

Certainly, they are not part of the New Testament canon. Although that canon was long debated, it has been well established for more than 1,500 years, and the re-introduction of the non-canonical texts to the canon is not likely to happen. However, this does not mean that these texts are not of value to communities of faith.

In a recent article on Mary Magdalene, Karen King, whose work we briefly examined in chapter 3, looks at the value of these texts. She emphasizes that as fairly new discoveries for scholars, they need to be thoroughly examined for what they can tell us about the role of women and the diversity of beliefs in the first several centuries of Christianity, as well as a variety of other issues. She also makes a curious observation about their theological value:

> To take the new texts seriously as historical documents does not mean considering them to be theologically authoritative for contemporary believers. *That determination has to be made—as it always has been—by communities of faith.* (Italics mine)

King reveals three things in these brief sentences. First, she insists that it is important to take these documents seriously as historical information, as they tell us much about forms of Christianity in its first several centuries. Second, she holds that to take them seriously as historical artifacts is not the same thing as considering them theologically authoritative. These are important points to make in establishing the task of a historian dealing with non-canonical texts, which is inquiry into the beliefs of an early community, not an unequivocal endorsement. However, in her third point, she does something a little different: Rather than unilaterally dismissing the theological value and authority of the non-canonical gospels, she leaves that determination up to the discretion of Christian communities. This strikes me as an incredible proposal that creates the possibility of a new place for the non-canonical gospels in the life of the church.

Although it seems that King certainly leaves open the possibility that the non-canonical gospels could become as authoritative as the canonical texts, I would think that many of the same organic criteria that prevented them from becoming canonical in the first place would still come into play. However, if these texts are used by communities of faith in ways that are mediated by the traditions and history of the faith, an awareness of the scholarship surrounding the non-canonical texts, and a willingness to be innovative in the ways we approach scripture, they can become powerful complements to the biblical texts communities of faith know so well, giving congregants fresh ways to read familiar stories. But what might that look like?

Clue Two: History and Story

I see two main ways the non-canonical gospels can be integrated into the life of a Christian community. First, if the Christian faith is a story that tells us something about who we are, that story can be complemented well by research into the historical context(s) that produced that story. The history of a movement can illuminate the stories it produces. Likewise, the stories we have collected, read, or rediscovered can tell us much about the historical circumstances surrounding a period in time. The non-canonical gospels, therefore, tell us much about the different strands of Christianity that were developing in the first several hundred years of the movement. These texts can help demonstrate some of the challenges facing the early churches as they struggled to establish their identities. These gospels become important tools in the search for early Christian movements, a search that, though mediated by biblical scholarship, ultimately weaves its way into the questions of history and identity that churches ask about themselves.

A second, more experimental, use of these texts draws on an old rabbinical interpretive practice known as *midrash.* From the Hebrew, meaning "to search" or "investigate," midrash is a type of scriptural commentary that offers new interpretations of well-known scriptural passages, often by retelling the story with additional details, passages of dialogue, or twists in the story. Midrash is often quite imaginative and theologically innovative. Though not considered part of the canonical scriptures, midrash is a resource for reflection on the Jewish scriptures, or *Torah*. Midrash is often described as a product of the prayerful consideration of a text or the result of a rabbi's dialogue with God concerning the meaning of a puzzling passage of scripture.

We know that many of the non-canonical texts were written much later than the canonical gospels and contain teachings that were innovative (though often heretical). Still, these non-canonical texts relied on the knowledge of earlier, accepted Christian traditions. Thus I propose that Christian communities begin to consider these non-canonical texts as a type of midrash.

I am not implying that these non-canonical gospels were written as midrash, though it is at least possible that they may have been engendered as companions or complements to other gospels. However, what if we began to read them as if they had midrashic value? Could *The Gospel of Mary* or *The Gospel of Thomas* have value for a Christian community other than as a resource for imagining the historical context in which the canon was debated?

For example, 1 Peter, like many of the other epistles, contains a set of household codes that orders wives to accept the authority of their husbands (particularly non-Christian husbands) so that they might be won over as converts:

> Wives, in the same way, accept the authority of your husbands, so that, even if some of them do not obey the word, they may be won over without a word by their wives' conduct, when they see the purity and reverence of your lives…It was in this way long ago that the holy women who hoped in God used to adorn themselves by accepting the authority of their husbands. (1 Pet. 3:1–2, 5)

In contemporary contexts, this passage has been used, as have similar codes and customs in Colossians and 1 Corinthians, to place women in a subjugated role in the life of the church and in familial relations. Second, though most scholars do not believe that this was actually written by Peter, it likely comes from a community that got its theological credence from relying on Peter as a patron disciple. Both *The Gospel of Thomas* and *The Gospel of Mary* feature a point in which Peter questions the authority of Mary based on her gender. Peter's false presumption is corrected in *Thomas* by Jesus and in *Mary* by Levi and by Mary herself. Read in such a way, these texts become interpretive tools in the life of Christian practice, helping elucidate, nuance, or critique points made in canonical texts and opening up new veins of discussion on issues such as gender roles and expectations in Christian communities.

Likewise, *The Gospel of Thomas*, though containing many of the sayings of Jesus found in the other gospels, often develops different themes around them or presents them in close proximity of other, unorthodox sayings. Read alongside the same sayings in canonical texts, they can function as commentary on what we hold as accepted scripture.

Other possibilities abound. The christology of *The Gospel of Philip* could enhance our reading of Mark. Discussions on table fellowship in the *Didache* could enhance our theological understanding of the words of institution found in the gospels and in 1 Corinthians 11. When mediated by responsible scholarship with a respect not only for the tradition preserved by the church but also for the history surrounding long-suppressed traditions, the possibilities for growth and innovation in the church are exciting.

Conclusion

One of the interesting issues raised by *The Da Vinci Code* is the existence of many gospels not included in the biblical canon. Much remains to be discovered concerning the interpretation of these texts and the context in which they were written. It is far from likely that any such texts will be added in any way to the church's authoritative canon. Still, these texts have the potential to illuminate the history surrounding the development of the early church and could potentially prove to be important resources for contemporary

Christian communities, whether in the study of their historical roots or as new resources for theological reflection.

What Do We Do with the Christian Story after *The Da Vinci Code*?

In *The Da Vinci Code*, Dan Brown wrote a great mystery. As we have seen through the six brief chapters of this book, however, he has taken significant liberties with history to make his story intriguing, and in parts, thrilling. In doing so, he has garnered the ire of not only those who believe in a literal interpretation of the Bible, but also of those who are committed to responsible representation of early Christian history.

But it's not that Brown gets every iota of history wrong. He draws on some very real events, such as the discovery of the Nag Hammadi texts and Constantine's patronage of the church, to create a sort of parallel world, a "What if?" scenario. He gives us an engrossing *fiction* that provides us with a few clues here and there that we must use to make sense of a mystery much greater than the plot of his novel reveals. To characterize Brown's work as a direct attack against the foundation of the Christian faith, or to name it as a weapon in some sort of culture war that threatens the sanctity of religion in the United States is to take *The Da Vinci Code* far too seriously. The same can be said for considering Brown's book to be a definitive discourse on two millennia of theological error and the church's cover-up.

What *The Da Vinci Code* does provide are clues to another mystery that Christians of all sorts have been struggling with from the very beginning of their faith. The hints that Brown gives toward the historical development of the church, the canon, the marginalization of women in the church, and especially the identity of Jesus raise serious questions being debated among Evangelicals, Mainline Protestants, Catholics, and all sorts of other types of Christians. In doing so, Brown sets his readers out to solve a more complex, more nuanced mystery than he probably imagined. This mystery is certainly original and unique—perhaps even core—to Christianity, and quite frankly, it is a mystery that takes a lifetime to answer.

By presenting people of faith with innuendo that demands investigation and hints that demand research into the origins of Christianity itself, Brown has set us down the path toward answering for ourselves the question that Jesus posed to his first disciples in the synoptic gospels:

"Who do *you* say that I am?"

DISCUSSION QUESTIONS

1. How do stories shape communities? Can you think of an example?
2. Has *The Da Vinci Code* affected how you look at Christianity?
3. Can Christians use a concept such as *midrash*? Does it make sense in the life of the church?
4. Has *The Da Vinci Code* been a helpful tool in your journey of faith?
5. What elements of the Christian story must be original for Christianity to be true?

For Further Reading

Barnstone, Willis, and Marvin Meyer. *The Gnostic Bible*. Boston: Shambhala, 2003.

Boyarin, Daniel. "Midrash." In *Handbook of Postmodern Biblical Interpretation,* ed. A. K. M. Adam. St. Louis: Chalice Press, 2000.

Duncan, David James. "When Compassion Becomes Dissent." *Orion Magazine.* January/February 2003.

Goodstein, Laurie. "Best Seller Has Some Christians on Defensive." *The New York Times,* 27 April 2004.

King, Karen. "Letting Mary Magdalene Speak." Article available on www.beliefnet.com